UFOs

ABOVE
THE LAW

UFOs

ABOVE THE LAW

*True Incidents of
Law Enforcement Officers'
Encounters with UFOs*

Frank Soriano

and

Jim Bouck

4880 Lower Valley Road, Atglen, Pennsylvania 19310

DEDICATION

We dedicate this book to those pilots, ufonauts, and or EBEs (extraterrestrial biological entities), whoever you are, and your fantastic, amazing, and awesome flying crafts commonly known as UFOs. If not for you, this book and any other endeavors connected with UFOs would not have been possible.

Text and images by authors unless otherwise noted

Schiffer Books are available at special discounts for bulk purchases for sales promotions or premiums. Special editions, including personalized covers, corporate imprints, and excerpts can be created in large quantities for special needs. For more information contact the publisher:

Published by Schiffer Publishing Ltd.
4880 Lower Valley Road
Atglen, PA 19310
Phone: (610) 593-1777; Fax: (610) 593-2002
E-mail: Info@schifferbooks.com

For the largest selection of fine reference books on this and related subjects,
please visit our website at
www.schifferbooks.com
We are always looking for people to write books on new and related subjects.
If you have an idea for a book, please contact us at
proposals@schifferbooks.com

This book may be purchased from the publisher.
Include $5.00 for shipping.
Please try your bookstore first.
You may write for a free catalog.

In Europe, Schiffer books are distributed by
Bushwood Books
6 Marksbury Ave.
Kew Gardens
Surrey TW9 4JF England
Phone: 44 (0) 20 8392 8585; Fax: 44 (0) 20 8392 9876
E-mail: info@bushwoodbooks.co.uk
Website: www.bushwoodbooks.co.uk

Designed by Mark David Bowyer
Type set in Palette / New Baskerville BT

ISBN: 978-0-7643-3920-2
Printed in the United States of America

CONTENTS

ACKNOWLEDGMENTS

There are a number of people that we would wish to thank and give our sincere appreciation for their inspiration and support in the writing of this book.

First and foremost, we can't show enough appreciation to our wives, Miriam Soriano and Lynn C. Bouck. The things that they have put up with during our meetings, research, and the time writing this is so much appreciated. They have stood behind us, encouraged us, and sometimes even pushed us. Thank you both.

Next, we want to thank retired optical physicist for the US Navy Department of Weapons Research, author and lecturer Dr. Bruce Maccabee for suggesting that we write this book in revealing our experiences and those of other law enforcement officers, and for his review and suggestions along the way.

Thanks also to retired nuclear physicist, author, lecturer, and UFO researcher Stanton T. Friedman for the many telephone conversations and for his support in seeing this book come to life.

Kathy Marden, thank you for the picture of your aunt and uncle, Betty and Barney Hill and for information needed, or missed by us and for your kind words.

Finally, we want to thank researcher, author and lecturer, Richard Dolan, and his wife, Karyn. Words cannot express our profound thanks for their confidence and work in proofreading and editing this book on a subject that we, and all of those mentioned, truly believe in. With all of our great intentions, we'd probably sound a little confusing had it not been for their encouragement and reviewing of our work. The amount of time Karyn put into reviewing and making sure we left out no references, identifications, and direction made us feel comfortable enough to put this book out before you. And further to Richard for his Foreword comments.

Another person who deserves special acknowledgement for contributing the idea for our book cover is Professor Dennis K. Anderson, astronomer and planetarium director for Wagner College, Staten Island, New York.

Thanks also to Dinah Roseberry, Senior Editor for the paranormal and mind/body/spirit divisions of Schiffer Publishing, LTD. This book would not exist if not for the trust and confidence from the Schiffer family. Thank you for opening the door.

Thank you to all who have helped us.

FOREWORD

BY RICHARD M. DOLAN

One thing about the UFO phenomenon is that it is persistent. Despite the repeated instances in which official pronouncements have decreed it to be a non-issue, it keeps coming back. Clearly, the operators of these "things" have not gotten the memo that they are not supposed to exist.

A key explanation offered for UFOs is that they are the result of observers misinterpreting normal events, some of which might be unusual, but all of which are ultimately prosaic. Ball lightning, temperature inversions, balloons, "Chinese lanterns," insects, birds, unusual aircraft, satellites, and scintillating stars are a few of the culprits, we are told, that account for the vast number of UFO reports, usually told by sincere people who just did not understand what they saw.

In fact, this is often the case. People *do* make mistakes. It is a truism – and entirely true – that around ninety percent of what people think to be UFOs are in fact quite ordinary things. When seeing something that seems as though it might be a UFO, most of us get excited. It can be hard, sometimes, not to jump to conclusions before turning the matter over fully in one's mind and considering all the alternatives, boring though they may be.

And yet, throughout the history of UFO sightings, there have always been cases that defy conventional explanations. Not all sightings have been of a vague, distant, nocturnal light. Many have been made in broad daylight. Many have been made at close range. Many have been tracked by electronic instrumentation. And still many more have been made by highly competent observers.

Which makes the subject of this book so very interesting.

Police officers may well be the epitome of the trained observer. Every day, their ability to observe correctly and rapidly can make the difference between life and death. And not only regarding the general public, but themselves.

One interesting fact about police officers is that they spend much of their time outside. Now, there are other professions – road workers, park rangers, mail carriers – where this is also true, but certainly we need our cops out on the streets where the action is. And when you are out on the streets, it's not hard to look up at the sky once in while.

I grew up among cops. My dad was a New York City police officer, as was one of my uncles. I knew most of my dad's partners, and when I got older, I got to play softball at a few police picnics. To me, cops have always been very interesting people. Don't try lying to an experienced cop. They know how to sniff out B.S. when it wafts their way. Many of them eventually become a bit jaded. After all, when you have been on the job long enough, you truly *have* "seen it all."

For that reason, they are often famously skeptical of UFOs (that is, of course, until they see one). During an intense wave of UFO sightings over Hudson Valley in the early 1980s, for example, one police officer told a nearly hysterical witness to "sleep it off and the pink UFO will go away." To be fair, this was before the advent of community policing, but – no question – that surely sounds like a cop.

But here's the thing. Because they are engaged with the public and the outside environment in ways that most of us are not, and because they are not easy to startle, and because they are specifically trained to be factual and precise observers, police officers are among the most qualified people around to observe UFOs. And it turns out that some of the best UFO reports we have are by police officers.

Especially so, when you consider that whenever somebody sees a UFO, their first phone call will nearly always go to the police. It's the cop on the beat who is called to do something about it.

To be sure, not every cop who has seen a UFO believes it was an alien spacecraft. In their public statements, most tend to avoid making a conclusion at all, frequently confining themselves simply to a statement of what they saw. But in most of these instances, it's quite obvious that they fully realized they saw something utterly extraordinary. Something that, for all they knew, was not supposed to exist.

This fascinating book tells a story that is long overdue. It is the story of our public servants – men and women who are charged with protecting our lives – and their encounters with *the impossible*.

Impossible, but real all the same.

Frank Soriano and Jim Bouck are well suited to their task. Frank is a retired New York State Corrections Officer, and Jim is a former New York State Park police officer. Both of these men truly have "seen it all" in the course of their careers. Each has also been a UFO witness – in Frank's case more than once. Both are extremely knowledgeable about the subject, and Jim was the New York State Director for the Mutual UFO Network – the largest and oldest UFO investigative organization in the United States.

I know both of these men personally, and have shared many hours of open, honest conversation with them. You cannot find two more dedicated and conscientious researchers.

And thorough. While some of the cases in this book are known to experienced students of UFOs, quite a few of these are fresh, at least to my knowledge. Somehow, they slipped through the cracks, but Frank and Jim have revived them here. Moreover, everything is presented in a calm, succinct, down-to-earth voice – rather what you would expect from two law enforcement professionals.

While this book serves as a wonderful reference, something that you could cherry pick, as it were, for the particular cases you find most interesting, it has a power when read straight through. The succession of powerful cases, of baffled witnesses, of shattered realities, leaves an overriding impression that we are most certainly not alone. That there is an intelligence interacting with our species, our world, that is practically screaming to get our attention.

I will leave it for you to answer what it means for a society to live in such a schizophrenic manner. One in which millions of people have interactions with an extremely advanced technology and intelligence, and in which at the same time, they are told by their authorities that there is nothing at all to see.

Frank Soriano and Jim Bouck have done us all a great service in writing this book. Yes, they have made a strong case for the reality of the UFO phenomenon. But they have also written a book that should be read by anyone involved in law enforcement. First, police officers – and those who are in the related professions who are represented here – will realize that many of their fellow professionals in the field have quietly seen something that has challenged their understanding of reality.

But this book will be especially cathartic for those officers who, like the authors, have seen a UFO. They will find cases like their own. They will find witnesses they can identify with. And they will find comfort in the knowledge that, just as we are not alone in the universe, they are not alone among their brothers and sisters in blue.

~Richard M. Dolan
Rochester, New York

INTRODUCTION

The idea of writing a UFO book witnessed by law enforcement officers was given to Frank Soriano by Dr. Bruce Macabbee, because of Frank's many personal UFO sightings during the time he worked in law enforcement.

When Frank and Jim first met in November of 1993, Frank and his wife were New York State Correction Officers. Frank started out in New York City and later moved to Ticonderoga, a small town in the Adirondacks near Lake Champlain. It is known as a popular tourist area and as the location of the historic Fort Ticonderoga. When he and his wife witnessed a UFO, he reported it to the Mutual UFO Network (MUFON), and thus met investigator Jim Bouck.

Jim worked as an auditor for the New York State Comptroller's Office, but had been a New York State police officer in the 1980s. When Frank reported his UFO sightings to Jim, the two men found a mutual bonding in their shared law enforcement background.

In 1982, Jim had become a police officer for New York State with the Palisades Interstate Park Police at Bear Mountain State Park, along the Hudson River about forty miles north of New York City. New York and New Jersey share jurisdiction over this area, along the Palisades Parkway down to Palisades Park. This area was made famous in the 1980s by a wave of UFO sightings, later recounted in *Night Seige: The Hudson Valley UFO Sightings* by Dr. J. Allen Hynek and Philip J. Imbrogno with Bob Pratt.

Also in Orange County, not too many miles from the Palisades Park region, is the area known as Pine Bush, New York. This area became well known in UFO literature in a book written by Ellen Crystal called *Silent Invasion,* about UFO sightings by most of the residents of the tiny town of Pine Bush, New York.

Jim was laid off from that job due to NYS budget cuts in 1983, just as the UFO wave began. Thus he missed out on some of the biggest UFO sightings and investigations in UFO history. He never had a UFO sighting himself until the year 2003.

THE APPROACH

Because of our law enforcement background, we approach the subject of UFO investigation in a different way than that adopted by many researchers. Police officers are trained to observe, to collect, and evaluate evidence in a way that the layman is not. All of these skills are brought to bear on the cases in this book. This collection is unique because all of the sightings here were reported to us by law enforcement officers, military police, and members of similar professions. These cases are not limited to the New York State area, but have come from around the world, thus proving that this phenomenon is widespread and worthy of careful investigation, despite the ridicule that it often receives in the media.

An important part of any investigation is establishing the credibility of the witness. In a field like UFO research, which many people find incredible to begin with, this becomes even more important. Experienced researchers have less trouble believing a witness than the scientific community does, or the uninformed general public who has never seen a UFO and only relies on what they had been taught in the growing and learning stages of their lives. As a result, many UFO sightings have gone unreported. To report a UFO sighting takes a lot of courage. For a witness who has a lot to lose by going public, seeing a UFO puts them in a very uncomfortable position. To see something and say nothing is a lot easier to do. By reporting a UFO sighting, you put yourself on exhibit. You can report the UFO and remain anonymous but then you didn't report the UFO, "anonymous" did, and few people consider this a credible source. Still this makes some witnesses nervous. By taking a stand and letting people see that you are the one reporting the UFO, you will take the chance of being ridiculed, and you can become a target. If you see the UFO with another witness, or something that others have seen and reported also, your chances of being attacked lessens. It's easier to make fun of one person than it is to make fun of a group. Therefore, in researching and investigating UFOs, we have no problems with someone who wishes anonymity. That is why we will either use no names, fictional names, or just first names of witnesses in this book unless the witness has been published before and his or her sighting is well known already.

The law enforcement officer who sees a UFO and keeps it to him- or herself will be able to continue life the way it was before the sighting, but the one who reports the UFO has to be aware of what lies ahead. The reason we are writing this book is to give that law enforcement officer a back up when confronted by the skeptical public or other officers. We hope to show that there are hundreds, and even thousands, of officers that see these objects and are not alone.

The fear of feeling inadequate, the lack of stamina, every time you see yourself in the mirror can be very disturbing. Keeping the truth to yourself is no different than telling a lie when you allow the lie to live with your silence.

It all depends on the persona of the individual. Does he or she have the guts or the intestinal fortitude to report the truth, or is he or she afraid to speak the truth?

In Frank Soriano's case, he got tired of hiding the truth about UFOs. He eventually asked himself, "Why am I hiding the truth?" He didn't feel right about himself. He felt inadequate, yet strange that as a correction officer while off duty, he could witness a murder and within an hour assist the Yonkers, New York detectives in the apprehension of the homicide suspect, and as the star witness, he would calmly testify against him to the Grand Jury. But for years, he could not bring himself to express the truth about the aircraft he was seeing of unknown origin, commonly referred to as Unidentified Flying Objects (UFOs), and that they were in fact real.

As for the patrol officer who is on duty and receives a dispatch call of strange lights in the sky acting oddly, this could put him into the path of a UFO sighting, leaving the officer with the decision to report or to ignore what he has just witnessed. What they may see is so incredible, fascinating, and even perplexedly terrorizing at times that some officers can't believe their eyes until other units see and report the same strange lights or craft from different areas of the city, county, or state, etc.

Since these reports are a major ingredient of the UFO enigma, and the law enforcement officers are trained to assess the situation logically, the credibility of such a sighting is vastly enhanced.

A STUNNING EVENT

To see a UFO is truly a stunning event. Even multiple sightings do not diminish the intensity of the emotional reaction. This feeling comes over you, because the UFO is there, you can clearly see it, and it has no known aircraft shape that you have ever seen before. Its appearance is unusual in shape and performance. To your amazement, this wingless craft is hovering silently in the sky, it's large and still. Your mind sends off a slew of questions: What is it? Where does it come from? What's holding that big thing up?

At this point, you're sorry you didn't bring your photo or video camera along which you could use as evidence of your sighting, proof of what you just witnessed. Wrong! It won't work. Photos and video tapes showing a crime being committed can and have been used in courts of

law with very good results as evidence, but such evidence concerning photos or videos of UFOs is explained away or rebuffed by government officials, skeptics, scientists, or other law enforcement officers. What's wrong with this picture?

To hold positions, they must be intelligent, perceptive individuals with a responsibility and allegiance toward the citizens of whom they serve. The citizens from all walks of life, here in America and throughout the world are not blind. Dark and grainy photographs and video film have been used and accepted with positive results in courts of law throughout the land, but sharp, clear, and distinct photos or video film footage of UFOs is explained away as something other than what it clearly is, a UFO!

Credible professionals such as airline and military pilots, police officers, politicians, doctors, lawyers, and others have submitted so many credible reports of UFO sightings. Thousands of these sightings are caught on film worldwide; these UFO sightings are not imaginary because one cannot capture his or her imagination on film. Yet, still the denial by officials continues, even though this is an intrusion of our air space by unidentified flying craft of unknown origin. Consider what we went through on September 11, 2001, when hijacked aircraft struck major buildings in several cities and resulted in the deaths of thousands of innocent people. You would think that if anything in our skies is seen by anyone, and cannot be completely and confidently identified, that it would be investigated to make sure that there isn't another such attack happening again.

It's strange that public citizens take this so much more seriously than the officials in high-ranking positions do. This isn't mass hysteria on a worldwide spectrum. This is mass fascination and curiosity by the people who want to know, and who have a right to know, the truth about UFOs.

Skeptics vigorously and constantly attempt to downplay important and credible sightings made by solid citizens, including professionals of law enforcement, who vastly outnumber their detractors. For more than fifty years, they have effectively used premeditated deceit and misinformation to discredit the whole subject of UFOs. The result is that most people, including our President, Vice President, Congress, and Senate, will engage in serious discussions of God and angels without ridicule or laughter, but not UFOs.

The question is, are these UFO reports and videos of them real or imaginary? One could argue that there is far more evidence of the existence of UFOs than of the existence of God. We believe in God and also in UFOs. In the past, most people were taught when they were young that such things as UFOs and ET beings don't exist. While that is still often the case, people today are more open-minded and independent in their thinking, more willing to consider evidence rather than blindly follow the beliefs of their childhood.

For years, the government and skeptics have exhausted themselves in trying to convince "normal intelligent people" that the UFO they just observed was "flares," "a helicopter," "the planet Venus," "the moon," "a star," conventional aircraft, and the list goes on. Many of these are daylight sightings, clearly seen, and many unidentified objects have been recorded on photos or videotape.

The most common explanation is that of misidentified conventional aircraft. It is a simple matter to compare an unidentified object with photographs and video photos of known aircraft. Unfortunately, skeptics will often attempt to use this explanation on objects that, on examination, simply don't resemble conventional aircraft at all. That's like trying to convince you that it wasn't a tank you saw, it was just a baby stroller! These pompous excuses or lies, whichever suit you, are an insult to the credible witnesses worldwide who have reported seeing objects which they were unable to identify. They evaporate the trust and confidence people once had for our government officials.

Further explanations for UFOs include weather balloons, atmospheric phenomena, light aberrations, mass hallucinations, hoaxes, swamp gas, and many more. Although these are all real objects that are often seen in the skies, they are also used as excuses for many sightings which truly do remain unidentified. This can often be proven by even a cursory examination of the evidence.

This is how the government explains away UFO sightings, regardless of who reports them. It's the government's and skeptics' labyrinth of lies that is most suitable for their purposes.

Authorities fear that acknowledging the existence of non-domestic advanced performance craft of unknown origin may cause worldwide panic. Something like that did occur after Orson Welles' rendition of *War of Worlds* on his radio broadcast in 1938, which vividly described an alien invasion of Earth. However, we are now far more advanced in scientific technology and mentally capable of dealing with new discoveries. Fear of widespread panic is no longer a good reason to keep such important information hidden from the public. We have lived through numerous wars, horrific terrorist attacks, and many other terrible events. Our government has made a point of informing the public of terrorist threats so that we can prepare to defend ourselves. Yes, people were frightened by this; but there was no widespread panic. When we see a UFO, our senses tell us that it is foreign, but we don't panic, we just look at it in amazement and wonderment.

Our government also claims that, for reasons of national security, most documents relating to UFOs cannot be released. That's fine, don't release them, but don't deny that there is something to them, and don't leave us unguarded and in the dark for lack of information about UFOs. Just acknowledge what we already know: that UFOs are foreign, they are not ours, you can't control their movements, and you don't know what their agenda is.

We are survivors and can endure, but only if we know what we are up against. The public assures national security by reporting these sightings, which should be considered a public service. Nevertheless, our government continues to state publicly that the subject of UFOs is nonsense and not worth serious scientific consideration. The US government is second to none in misinforming the public about UFOs, because we have the habit of believing and trusting in what they say. (Do you think other countries trust their governments less? Are other governments more or less trustworthy than the US government?)

WHY DENY?

Why deny the existence of UFOs? The reason may very well be that after years of study on the subject matter, it is clear that these foreign crafts are so far in advance of our own technology that we have no defense against them. There is absolutely nothing our government can do to stop these UFOs from entering our airspace at will, so they simply refuse to acknowledge the existence of these objects. By refusing to admit our helplessness, public trust and faith in government remains intact. So the denial and cover-up will continue until something occurs which leaves authorities with no choice but to finally come clean about UFOs.

Another theory may be that the money being put into the secret programs, known as "black ops" funds, may be coming from private sources. When alien technology is studied and new breakthroughs are made, these private sources may want to claim ownership of the new information and inventions for their own use, or for the profits that can result from their sale.

In this book you will find a number of references to Dr. J. Allen Hynek. Briefly, Dr. Hynek was an astronomer at Northwestern College when he was recruited to be a part of the Air Force group known as Project Blue Book, which was the government's attempt to show the American public that it really wanted to look into the subject of UFOs and find out what was happening. Dr. Hynek's job was to help refute the claim that UFOs (known at that time as Flying Saucers) were conventional objects and were the result of nothing more than misidentifications or wild imaginations. However, during the course of his research, Dr. Hynek began to see that some of the witnesses were very credible, unlikely to make things up or mistakenly identify what they were observing. He began to suspect that there may actually be something to this phenomena, and after the demise of Project Blue Book, he organized a UFO research group known as the Center for UFO Study (CUFOS) to continue the work that was no longer being done officially by the Air Force.

From this point on, we will present reports from what we feel are the most credible witnesses; and you the reader can make up your mind as to your conclusion based on the evidence presented in the following chapters of this book.

QUOTES

"It was a little bit scary. It makes you wonder. If it is something from outer space and hasn't bothered anybody and you start bothering them, and if they're intelligent enough to get down here, no telling what they could do to you."

~Patrolman Howard Dellinger
During a helicopter patrol over Charlotte, North Carolina 12/27/1977 while trying to track down a UFO

"It was about as long as a football field and fifty to seventy-five yards wide."

~Patrolman Troy Todd
Two tactical squad patrolmen who spotted a UFO while on patrol in an unmarked police car in Memphis, Tennessee
May 17, 1977

(He and his partner, Patrolman Jerry Jeter, were definitely impressed.)

"I got out of the cruiser and went into the field and all of a sudden this thing came at me at about 100 feet off the ground with red lights going back and forth. Officer Hunt got there and also saw this thing. It had no motor and came through the air like a leaf falling from the tree."

~From police report by Ptl. E. Bertrand
Exeter, New Hampshire
September 3, 1965

(By the time Hunt got to this field, the UFO had gone over the trees, but he saw it.)

"We estimated that the UFO came within 450 to 500 yards of us when we flashed our lights." It scared the living tar out of me. I felt in danger of my life and I guess I panicked. I shouted at my partner to turn off our lights and the craft backed off."

~*National Enquirer*
October 22, 1974

"Condemnation without investigation is the height of ignorance."

~Albert Einstein

"It was the damnedest thing I've ever seen. It was big, it was very bright, it changed colors and it was about the size of the moon. We watched it for ten minutes, but none of us could figure out what it was. One thing's for sure, I'll never make fun of people who people who say they've seen unidentified objects in the sky."

~Former US President, Jimmy Carter From the DVD – *UFO: Top Secret*
As seen on Sci-Fi and TLC channels

"I was in a plane last week when I looked out the window and saw this white light. It was zigzagging around. We followed it for several minutes. It was a bright white light. We followed it to Bakersfield, and all of a sudden, to our amazement, it went straight up into the heavens. When we got off the plane, I told Nancy all about it."

~Former US President, Ronald Reagan
From the DVD – *UFO: Top Secret*
As seen on Sci-Fi and TLC channels

"We're ordered to hide sightings when possible, but if a strong report does get out, we have to publish a fast explanation – make up something to kill the report in a hurry and to ridicule the witness, especially if we can't figure out a plausible answer. We even have to discredit our own pilots. It's a raw deal, but we can't buck the CIA. The whole thing makes me sick. I'm thinking of putting in for inactive."

~Captain Edward J. Ruppelt, US Air Force Project Blue Book

"I believe that these extraterrestrial vehicles and their crews are visiting this planet from other planets, which obviously are a little more technically advanced than we are here on Earth. For many years I have lived with a secret, in a secrecy imposed on all specialists and astronauts. I can now reveal that every day, in the USA, our radar instruments capture objects of form and composition unknown to us."

~Gordon Cooper
Astronaut and the last American to fly in space alone

"The ignorance of consequence is the consequence for ignorance."

~Frank Soriano

"What we once believed to be true may not necessarily be true."

~Jim Bouck

"We seek a free flow of information... we are not afraid to entrust the American people with unpleasant facts, foreign ideas, alien philosophies, and competitive values. For a nation that is afraid to let its people judge the truth and falsehood in an open market is a nation that is afraid of its people."

~John F. Kennedy
November 21, 1963
Quoted on www.Presidentialufo.com)

"As my mind tried to register what I was looking at, the ball of light exploded in a blinding flash. Shards of light and particles fell into the fog. Several cops ran into the woods. I couldn't move: I tried to cover my eyes, but it was too late. Now right in front of me was a machine occupying the spot where the fog had been."

~Larry Warren
Former USAF security specialist

"I am aware that hundreds of military and airline pilots, airport personnel, astronomers, missile trackers, and other competent observers have reported these sightings… These UFOs are interplanetary devices systematically observing the earth, either manned or under remote control or both."

~Admiral Roscoe Hillenkoetter
First director of CIA, 08/22/1960

"The mind of UFOs is above our Universe."

~Jacob Soriano Bentley
3rd grader, grandson of Frank Soriano

What is a UFO?

Strictly speaking, a UFO is an Unidentified Flying Object. It is any object seen in the sky that cannot be positively identified. However, just being classified as a UFO does not mean that the object is extraterrestrial or inter-dimensional. All it means is that at that time of observation you just don't know what it is. In most cases, a UFO can be explained with a little research. Some of these things are planets such as Venus or Mars, airplanes, meteorites, balloons, stars, satellites, and the list goes on. At night most anything might look unidentified, especially depending on the angle from which it is seen and what lights might be visible. A commercial airplane must always have running lights on at night. When looking at one coming towards you, there will be a green light on the left wing and a red light on the right, and a white light may be in the middle of the front or back. When the plane is going away from you, it will be just the opposite, but remember that you might not be able to see all of the control lights all of the time. A check with the local airport air traffic control tower will tell you if someone was authorized to fly in the vicinity and picked up on radar.

Airplanes also make noise and must keep moving, except for helicopter and the Harrier Jet. These can hover, but they make a lot of noise. By contrast, UFOs are often silent and erratic in their movements, sometimes remaining still then moving in sudden bursts of high speed, and often maneuvering in ways that our conventional aircraft cannot.

UFOs are often reported in many different shapes and colors. They may be triangular, oval, round, ball shaped, cigar shaped, rod shaped and many others. There may be more than one object seen at a time, or just a light seen at night. In the Hudson Valley area of New York State, in the 1980s, the UFOs seen were large triangular or boomerang shaped. In Phoenix, Arizona, and over Oneida Lake, New York, during the 1990s, the UFOs were lights spread out across the sky. During World War II, many pilots reported seeing balls of lights that were nicknamed "foo fighters." These balls flew along side the planes and sometimes flew right into the plane and out again.

UFOs are reported at times to make no noise, fly and then stop in midair, or change directions, reverse direction without slowing down or stopping, or just to hover over an area.

Daylight Disk – A daylight disk, as its name implies, is a disk seen during the daylight hours (although the object does not have to be disk shaped.) Many objects have been reported to be seen during the day time and still the object remains unidentified.

Nocturnal Lights – Nocturnal lights, as opposed to the day light disk, is a light or series of lights that are seen at night. This is the most common type of UFO sighting reported, probably because the light against the dark sky draws attention while moving. This is also the hardest UFO to identify, because there is so little information to draw on when no part of the object can be seen but the light.

Lights seen in the sky at night seem to play an awful lot of games for those who watch them. Not that anyone is doing anything on purpose, but when you are not used to looking at the night sky for lights and not too familiar with the kinds of lights seen at night, it is easy to become confused. This is well-illustrated by an experience Jim had a few years ago.

Jim: I was doing a sky watch with some other UFO investigators at the Croton Falls Reservoir in New York State. We had been sitting all night alongside the road which runs through the reservoir. About 4 o'clock a.m., we noticed a light rising up slowly from behind a large hill across the reservoir from us. To say we were excited to see something would be an understatement. The light, as it was slowly moving higher in the sky would begin to move to the left and then to the right. It kept doing this. We all saw the same thing. However, looking into a pair of binoculars to get a better look at the object resulted in a disappointing discovery. I associated the placement of the light with a tree on the ground so as to see how much movement there was. I quickly learned that there was no movement of the light at all. It was just moving straight up very, very slowly. What had happened was, we were so determined to see a UFO, or at least hope to see one, that when a light we didn't expect came over the crest of the hill, we jumped to conclusions. It happens to lots of people lots of times. We looked at a star map and realized that the light was Venus. Staring at a light against a dark background will make it look like its moving. It's an optical illusion known as auto kinesis.

Sometimes UFOs are hoaxed. Either the witness has been deceived, or the person who reports a UFO may actually be the one responsible for the hoax. This has happened many times. A plastic bag with a candle in it will float, and the glowing light will create the effect of a UFO, or some one might attach a small flashlight or road flare to a high, flying kite. There are many ways to create the illusion of a UFO. Many other attempts have been tried.

Even photographs have been faked to get someone to fall prey to a hoax. Fortunately, we have some pretty good photo analysts available to weed out the phonies. Unfortunately, some still get by once in a while.

UFO Sightings

Before we get into the reports by law enforcement officers, let's look at some well-known reports in UFO history. This is not an all inclusive listing, but will show that this is a phenomenon that is being seen by many people from all over the world.

UFOs have been claimed to have a history as old as time itself. Some people say that the Bible has many recorded instances of Unidentified Flying Objects, and that the accounts of Ezekiel's wheel and Jacob's ladder were actually sightings of UFOs.

A painting by Lorenzo Della Fontana depicts the Madonna and two infants. In the background of the painting are a man and a dog looking up into the sky at what appears to be a UFO.

Kenneth Arnold

On June 24, 1947, a Boise, Idaho businessman and pilot named Kenneth Arnold was returning from a business trip when he learned of a search party for a downed Marine 4-46 transport plane that had been reported down somewhere in the Cascade Mountains. Arnold decided to take some time and see if he could spot it from the air. As he was flying, he noticed a flash of light off into the distance near Mt. Rainier.

While he tried to figure out what the light was, he saw it again. This time he watched it carefully and was able to determine that it was caused by the reflection of the sun off nine objects flying through the mountain range. The objects swerved around mountain peaks and flew in a formation of two parallel rows of four and five "craft" respectively. Arnold triangulated their speed between Mt. Rainier and Mt. Adams, and was astonished to learn that the objects were traveling at a speed of about 1,600 MPH, nearly three times as fast as any other aircraft of those days.

Kenneth Arnold gave a press conference at the airport when he landed and told the media what he had observed. He described the objects as "flat like a pie pan and so shiny they reflected the sun like a mirror."

He said their movements were comparable to those of "speedboats on rough water" and "like a saucer would (move) if you skipped it across the water." This incident led to the term *flying saucer* becoming a household name for these objects.

ROSWELL, NEW MEXICO

According to an article in the *Roswell Daily Record*, a local newspaper in Roswell, New Mexico, on July 8, 1947, the Army Air Force announced to the world that they had recovered a flying saucer. The article began:

> The intelligence office of the 509th Bombardment group at Roswell Army Air Field announced at noon today, that the field has come into possession of a flying saucer.
>
> According to information released by the department, over authority of Major J. A. Marcel, intelligence officer, the disk was recovered on a ranch in the Roswell vicinity, after an unidentified rancher had notified Sheriff Geo. Wilcox, here, that he had found the instrument on his premises.
>
> Major Marcel and a detail from his department went to the ranch and recovered the disk, it was stated.

However, the next day, the army Air Force announced that they had made a mistake and they had recovered a parachute and not a flying saucer. Apparently, they wanted us to think that a man who is both a Major and an Intelligence Officer in the United States Army Air Force, was unintelligent enough and inexperienced enough to mistake a parachute and a flying saucer.

Did a UFO crash on that farm near Roswell? If not, why did the military go through so much trouble to cover it up? They eventually even admitted that they lied on two separate occasions about this event. Witnesses claim that the military even had gone so far as to threaten their lives.

LUBBOCK LIGHTS

In 1951, an employee of the Atomic Energy Commission and his wife were sitting in their backyard in Albuquerque, New Mexico, when they observed a wing-shaped UFO fly over their heads. The object was about 1,000 feet above and had bluish-green lights. The object was also seen over Lubbock, Texas, by three college professors at 9:10 p.m. on

the same night. Shortly after that, three women in Lubbock also claimed to have seen this object. A few days later, a young college student, while lying in bed and looking out his window, saw similar lights and took a photograph of them.

The Air Force tried to explain this event away, but was unable to. There were simply too many credible witnesses. Over the next few weeks, they all reported seeing the same object and its lights. The professors saw this object over a dozen times over the next few months and was accompanied by many other witnesses. One explanation was that these sightings were just lights being reflected off the breasts of birds flying overhead. The witnesses refuted this claim stating that the object was too large, and flying too fast to be birds. Witnesses also claimed to have occasionally seen the object flying over clouds in the sky.[1]

BETTY AND BARNEY HILL

On September 19, 1961, a couple was driving home from a short but needed vacation at Niagara Falls. Betty and Barney Hill (a school teacher and postal worker, respectively) lived in Portsmouth, New Hampshire and had driven down Route 3 from Canada to their home. On their drive, they determined that they should be home at around 2:30 in the morning, 3 a.m. at the latest. While they were driving down the road, somewhere past the town of Colebrook near the town of Lancaster, Betty noticed a light in the sky that she thought was a planet near where the moon was situated. She watched the light as it seemed to be following them. She brought it to Barney's attention, but he shrugged it off as an airplane. Betty became concerned and took out a pair of binoculars to observe it. She kept mentioning it to Barney, who acted like he was

Betty and Barney Hill. *Courtesy of Kathleen Marsden.*

paying little attention to it so as not to trouble Betty, although he later admitted that he was becoming concerned himself. Eventually, to satisfy Betty, Barney pulled over to the side of the road in the White Mountain area of New Hampshire. He took the binoculars from Betty and got out of the car. The object was still coming in closer to them. Barney could see the object now quite clearly with the binoculars and thought that it was about the size of the distance between three telephone poles.

Barney began to move slowly out into a field to get a better look. The object now had moved to about fifty feet from him and about the height of a single tall tree. He could see that it had two rows of windows and was longer than jet airliner. He saw that there were at least a half dozen beings looking at him from one of the windows. At one point, all but one moved from the window to a panel. They were doing something and the one was still looking at him. Betty began to scream to him to return to the car. He had a feeling that they were going to be captured so he ran to the car, got in, and quickly drove off.

As they were driving down the road, they heard a beeping noise and felt a strange tingling sensation, and began to feel drowsy. Sometime later, they remember hearing the beeping sound again. They realized that they were near the town of Concord, New Hampshire and were not too far from home. They arrived home just after dawn shortly after 5 a.m. After a brief breakfast snack, they went to bed and didn't get up again until about 3 p.m.

They had hoped to soon forget the past night's experience, but didn't realize that they were going to be tossed into the limelight of the world of ufology. The experience of Betty and Barney Hill is the first well-documented abduction case, and can be read in detail in John G. Fuller's book, *The Interrupted Journey* (Berkley, 1966.)[2] and the latest book by Kathleen Marden (Betty and Barney's niece) and Stanton Friedman titled *Captured: The Betty and Barney Hill UFO Experience*. (Published by New Page Publishers.)

UFOs Fly Over Washington, D.C.

On July 20, 1952, pilots on two separate airlines reported seeing objects flying over the Capitol area which is considered a no-fly zone for aircraft. Both pilots reported seeing three objects lit by bright lights. The air traffic controllers at the Washington National Airport reported that they had picked up eight objects on the radar.

According to an *Associated Press* article on the 21st, the objects were reported moving about 100 to 130 MPH and moving up and down. When the objects disappeared, it was reported that they were to have moved away at a speed of 7,000 MPH. (*UFOs and the National Security State*). The Air Force reported that they received no reports and no jets were sent out to investigate.

The following week, on the 26th, more sightings of about a dozen objects were seen flying over the Capitol again. This time the Air Force scrambled jets to intercept the objects after having been notified by the air traffic controller with the Civil Aeronautics Administration. The radar again confirmed that they were able to pick up objects in the sky as they

directed the jets toward the objects. Pilots reported seeing lights in the sky about ten miles ahead of them. As the jets attempted to overtake them, the objects simply disappeared.[3]

Hudson Valley Sightings

From the end of 1982 until the late 1980s, a number of UFO sightings caused a great stir of attention and excitement in the area just north of New York City. From New Haven, Connecticut, to the Pine Bush area of New York State, from Westchester and going as far north to Kingston, New York, over an estimated 500 witnesses reported seeing UFOs. Witnesses included police officers, members of the clergy, politicians, pilots, doctors, presidents of large corporations, and many others.

In the book *Night Siege* by Dr. J. Allen Hynek, Philip Imbrogno, and Bob Pratt, these witnesses described the object they saw as having a large triangular or boomerang shape, estimated at about 300 to 900 feet in length.

Skeptics claimed that what the witnesses were seeing was simply a group of ultra light planes flying in formation as a practical joke. Witnesses pointed out that the object was seen hovering, which proved that it was not an ultra light, as this type of aircraft must keep moving at all times or fall.

Phoenix Lights

January 22, 1997
Lights were first seen over the Phoenix, Arizona area by a medical doctor named Lynne Kitei, who quickly grabbed her camera and took some pictures of it. She then reported the sighting, and has since written a book about her experience.

March 13, 1997
Thousands of people throughout the Phoenix, Arizona area watched as lights slowly moved across the city and surrounding area.

One person who saw the lights, did not immediately come forward to admit he was the Governor of Arizona himself, Fyfe Symington. During all of the commotion caused by the lights, the media, researchers in the area, and Governor Symington set up a press conference to address the situation. During the conference, an aide came out onto the press floor dressed up in an alien costume and in handcuffs. He was led off the floor by police officers and a joke was made of the whole thing.

The Governor admitted that he had set up the press conference for this skit because too much attention was being paid to the lights, and he wanted to release some of the tension by making light of the situation. It seemed that the Governor did not believe that the lights were unexplained and wanted to put an end to it all. However, years later, when he was no longer in office, former Governor Symington admitted that he had seen the lights. He did not believe that they were flares, or anything else that was from *here*, and that it was a structured UFO.

MILITARY SIGHTINGS

Although military personnel are often told not to speak at any time of the incidents involving UFOs that they have witnessed or have even heard about, many have done so just the same. This book will contain numerous stories of sightings that men and women in our military have spoken out on. The following article is a brief example.

Former airmen reveal…

U.S. FIGHTER PILOTS HAVE
CHASED SCORES OF UFOS

A former Air Force veteran (name withheld) served twelve of his twenty years in the service as a radar operator and then became a police officer in Phillips, Wisconsin. After he left the service, he spoke out about the many UFO sightings that he and his colleagues experienced.

"When I was stationed in the Upper Peninsula of Michigan, we had whole groups of UFOs. We tracked them on radar and scrambled jets after them that chased them around the sky. Over a period of 12 years, I'd say I tracked at least 50 UFOs," he said.

When asked if any of the jets ever caught up with the UFOs, he replied, "No. Our jets would go up to around 52,000 feet, their normal limit, and the pilots would report the UFOs were 30,000 to 40,000 feet still higher." This would put the objects at an approximate altitude of 80,000 to 90,000 feet, far beyond our capabilities.

National Enquirer
April 20, 1976

(Many see the *National Enquirer* as an unreliable source. However, some UFO researchers have found evidence that it may have been used to release accurate information in a way that would prevent the public from believing it.)

RAF BENTWATERS AND RAF WOODBRIDGE
RENDLESHAM FOREST, SUFFOLK, ENGLAND

Starting on the day after Christmas in 1980, lights were seen in a wooded area of the Rendlesham Forest just outside the Woodbridge RAF/USAF Base over a period of three consecutive nights. Bentwaters RAF was one of the largest NATO air bases in England, and was only about two miles from the Woodbridge base.

The first night, a light was seen moving into the Rendlesham Forest by two security police officers. They watched the light while it moved into the wooded area, and immediately called the information in to the base. Two other security officers met with them at the East Gate where they were stationed. One of the officers stayed on patrol while the other went into the forest with the two new arrivals. They reported that they observed a conical or pyramid-shaped object with lights. As the men got closer to the object, it rose into the air and took off.

The next day, a team of officers went out into the wooded areas where the object had been seen, and found some markings on the ground that looked like landing marks.

That night, after they found the markings on the ground, and into the next morning, a team of officers led by the Deputy Base Commander Col. Charles Halt went back into the forest. During this time, the officers visually observed the object return. More officers were brought onto the scene as the night progressed. (http://www.ufoevidence.org/documents/doc661.htm)

Larry Warren was a member of the USAF Security Police, stationed at RAF Bentwaters base and was involved in these events. In his book (co-written with Peter Robbins), *Left At East Gate*, he gives the following descriptions of the events that occurred on the third day.

On December 28, 1980, Larry Warren returned to the base after a day off and immediately took up his duties as security officer on his post. During his shift, he overheard commotion from other security police on the radio about something strange being seen. Shortly thereafter, a truck pulled up to Warren and he was relieved from his post and ordered to get ready to go out into the nearby forest with the other officers. Larry didn't know yet what they were going into the forest for, and little did he know what they were going to experience.

When they left the base, there were two law enforcement cars and three pickup trucks with security police officers in them. They drove to the RAF Woodbridge Base and were given further directions, which led them into the Rendlesham Forest.

When they stopped, Larry could see many other security officers at the site. Some had already entered the forest further as he waited for his orders. He did notice one airman crouched down with his head in his hands and crying. In the forest, he noticed other officers waving flashlights around. He saw an open field with a fence. They started to move into the field, and as they entered it, he could see some ground fog. He noticed that there were other men near the fog area taking pictures and checking the area out with Geiger counters.

He overheard a radio transmission that repeated several times, "Here it comes, here it comes." Then he looked out across the field where he saw a red light approaching the area. He immediately thought it was a plane, but he could hear no sound and it was coming in too fast. It came in and hovered about twenty feet in the air above the patch of ground fog. It appeared to be only about the size of a basketball. Larry now realized that his own movements seemed very slow. He could barely raise his arm to look at his watch, but managed to see that the time was 1:30 a.m.

As he watched, the ball of light seemed to explode in a blinding flash, shards of light falling into the fog. He wanted to run away, but was unable to move. Where the fog had been was now a machine, shaped like a pyramid with a small red glow at the top. It was very hard to watch because of the brightness of the lighted object. The body of the object was white and at the bottom were two bright blue lights. The body seemed to be changing shape.

Larry was ordered, with a couple of others, to approach the object slowly. They got to a spot within about ten feet from it and then moved a little to the left and then to the right. He could barely see the object even then, as it seemed to get blurry. One man was checking it out with a Geiger counter; then they were ordered back to their original spot, about twenty-five feet away from the object.

Standing next to Larry were two English policemen. One was taking pictures. An airman was ordered to take the camera away from him.

Another light suddenly appeared from behind the object, and moved slowly to about ten feet away from it. Larry and the others could now see small creatures, which Larry thought at first were children. The beings approached the commanding officer and gave him something. Larry could not see what it was. Soon Larry and some of the others were told to return to their trucks and they left the scene.

The following is a copy of a memo written by Lt. Colonel Charles Halt on January 13, 1981, describing the events:

To: RAF/CC

1. Early in the morning of 27 Dec 80 (approximately 0300L) two USAF
   security police patrolmen saw unusual lights outside the back gate

at RAF Woodbridge. Thinking an aircraft might have crashed or been forced down, they called for permission to go outside the gate to investigate.... The individuals reported seeing a strange glowing object in the forest. The object was described as being metallic in appearance and triangular in shape, approximately two to three meters across the base and approximately two meters high. It illuminated the entire forest with a white light. The object itself had a pulsing red light on top and a bank(s) of blue lights underneath. The object was hovering or on legs. As the patrolmen approached the object it maneuvered through the trees and disappeared. At this time the animals on a nearby farm went into a frenzy. The object was briefly sighted approximately an hour later near the back gate.

2. The next day, three depressions 1 1/2" deep and 7" in diameter were found where the object had been sighted on the ground. The following night (29 Dec 80) the area was checked for radiation. Beta/Gamma readings of 0.1 mill roentgens were recorded with peak readings in the three depressions and near the center of the triangle formed by the three depressions. A nearby tree had moderate (0.05 - 0.07) readings on the side of the tree facing towards the three depressions.

3. Later in the night a red sun-like object was seen through the trees. It moved about and pulsed. At one point it appeared to throw off glowing particles and then broke into five separate white objects and disappeared. Immediately thereafter, three star like objects were noticed in the sky, two objects to the north and one to the south, all of which were about 10 degrees off of the horizon. The objects moved rapidly in sharp, angular movements and displayed red, green and blue lights. The objects to the north appeared to be elliptical through 8-10 power lens. They then turned to full circles. The objects in the north remained in the sky for an hour or more. The object to the south was visible for two to three hours and beamed down a stream of light from time to time. Numerous individuals, including the undersigned, witnessed the activities in paragraphs 2 and 3.

~Charles Halt *(signed)*
Charles I. Halt. Lt Col, USAF
Deputy Base Commander[4]

POLICE REPORTS

LONNIE ZAMORA

On April 24th, 1964, a police sergeant in the city of Socorro, New Mexico, was pursuing a speeder when he unexpectedly and unintentionally became the most famous policeman in UFO history. Sgt. Lonnie Zamora was chasing a speeding car along a rural road just outside of Socorro when he heard a loud roar in the sky and looked up to see a flaming object flying across the sky. Being a dedicated policeman, Zamora wanted to get his quota of speeding tickets; but knowing that there was a dynamite shack nearby and that the object might be the result of an explosion at the shack, he abandoned his chase to investigate.

He drove his patrol car as far up the mountain road as he could until he observed up ahead of him along side the road what at first looked like the site of a car accident, with what appeared to be a white car standing up on its end along the side of the road. He also saw what looked like two children wearing white coveralls near the vehicle. On second look, he realized that this was no ordinary motor vehicle accident. What he had thought was a car was egg shaped and sitting on four legs embedded into the ground.

Sgt. Zamora radioed the Sheriff's office for assistance. He then got out of his patrol car to approach the vehicle. As he left his car, the two "children" saw him and ran into the object. It then began to lift off the ground, as if it were about to fly away. As it lifted, he heard a loud roar and saw flames coming from the object, and he realized that this was the flaming object he had seen earlier. Afraid that it might explode, Zamora moved behind his car for protection and watched as it flew out of sight.

A New Mexico State policeman soon arrived to assist Zamora with the accident call. By the time he arrived, the object was already gone. There was only Zamora's word for what had happened – except for four marks on the ground where the object had rested its four legs, and a nearby bush that had been singed by the flames.

When the Air Force investigated this sighting as part of Project Blue Book, they attempted to discredit Lonnie Zamora and his report. In his book *The UFO Experience* by J. Allen Hynek, an astronomer assigned to the Air Force UFO investigation group, Hynek stated:

> My original investigation, directed towards breaking apart Zamora's account by seeking mutual contradictions in it and also by seeking to establish Zamora as an unreliable witness were fruitless. I was impressed by the high regard in which Zamora was held by his colleagues, and I personally am willing today to accept his testimony as genuine, particularly as it does fit a global pattern.

Hynek also mentioned that in his investigation he had encountered an unidentified witness who told him of what he saw while stopping at a local gas station north of town. The witness mentioned that he saw an object, flying toward the south, that he thought must have been in trouble and heading for a landing spot. He thought this because he could see a police car going out across the sandy terrain toward it.[5]

POMPTON LAKE, NEW JERSEY

January 11, 1966
The mayor of Wanaque, New Jersey, his son and two city patrolmen witnessed a glowing object at the reservoir at Pompton Lake during the night. The object maneuvered slowly over the reservoir and sent down a beam of light which melted a hole in the ice on the reservoir.

The next morning, at about 2 a.m., two other police officers radioed that they were watching the same "thing" over the reservoir and it was also making holes in the ice with beams of light. This time the object was also seen by two mayors, reservoir guards, police, and hundreds of civilian witnesses.[6]

SKOWHEGAN, MAINE

February 11, 1966
While riding on patrol through the town, two policemen stopped the patrol car to watch a brightly colored orange object hovering over the ground about a block away from them. They radioed in to report it and continued watching until it moved out of sight behind some buildings. *The Bangor Daily Newspaper* called the Dow Air Force Base

0 0 0

to see if they had any information on the sighting on their radar and were told that they did not. However, it was later reported on the police blotter that the police department had called to ask the same thing, and were told that there had been some blips on the radar at the same time in that vicinity.[7]

THOUSANDS IN MICHIGAN OBSERVE CAVORTING UFOS

Early on Sunday morning on March 27, 1966, a police officer in Bad Axe, Michigan, saw a UFO hovering over Lake Huron. He reported the object as being very large and moving too fast to be a star. Also seeing the object was a State Trooper and a Sheriff's Deputy from Huron County.

The previous night, thousands of calls were made to various police and radio stations about lights being observed over Hillsdale County just north of Ohio.

On March 20th, a number of sightings were made in Hillsdale and Dexter, Michigan. These sightings were quickly written off by the Air Force and Professor J. Allen Hynek, an Astrophysicist for Northwestern University who claimed that these witnesses were just seeing "swamp gas." This explanation bothered a number of the witnesses.

A Civil Defense Director for Hillsdale County was one of the critics of this explanation. "I don't know what it was, nor do the people who saw it, but this is trying to explain it away arbitrarily," he said. "The Air Force is going to get into trouble going on in this way. It seems a whitewash."

Another critic of this explanation was the Sheriff of Washtenaw County whose deputies have had several sightings.[8]

POMPTON LAKE, NEW JERSEY

October 1966

Late one night, a woman called the Wanaque Police Department to report that she had seen an object fly between her home on a mountain top and a cable antenna, and move down toward the reservoir. A police sergeant went to investigate. When he got there, he radioed in that he was watching an object about the size of an automobile hovering over the reservoir at about 150 feet. When he turned on his flashing red lights, the lighted object just blacked out and disappeared. It was witnessed a short time later from the Reservoir Police headquarters. [9]

UFO SEEN OVER UNIVERSITY OF CINCINNATI CAMPUS

A UFO was seen by six police officers over the University of Cincinnati Campus on April 17, 1968, at 12:30 a.m. The object was cone-shaped, about 12 feet tall and about 10 feet at its widest point, and its altitude was calculated at about 200 feet throughout the event. One officer said that it had a rocking motion like a buoy on a river. The object made no noise. It moved in a weaving manner and hovered over Sawyer Hall. The object moved with its broad end of the cone down, and had a bright light at the bottom and a red glow at the point. The light from the object switched from a bright glow to a dim glow. The light was as brilliant as a street arc light and moved in defiance of prevailing winds.

It was seen moving about 100 feet east and then about 200 feet west and then hovered before moving "at supersonic speed" in a southeasterly direction until it was out of sight. One report claimed the object seen was a plastic bag with a can of Sterno (a flammable gel used by campers for heat and cooking) inside, and this explanation seemed bolstered by the discovery of such a can on the campus grounds. However, the police report stated that six police officers witnessed the object, and were very clear that the object was far too large to be explained in this way.[10]

CRAWFORD, NEW YORK

January 4. 1971
A whirring turbine-like sound awakened a local police officer. He glanced out the window and saw a UFO hovering several hundred feet from his house. It was disc-shaped, silvery, and about 100 feet in diameter with a row of windows around a domed top. It was visible for about forty minutes, pulsating dull green to red.[11]

CHATHAM, NEW YORK

October 1973
A Police officer and over a dozen other witnesses watched six objects shaped like vertical carrots. The sighting lasted for more than an hour.[12]

GLOVERSVILLE, NEW YORK

October 17, 1973

About sixteen witnesses, including a policeman, saw a UFO with rotating red, blue, and off-white to amber lights. It remained stationary, quite high in the sky for possibly a half-hour. It began drifting slowly toward Earth and then shot down at high speed. After some forty minutes, the object darted horizontally in a northeasterly direction and disappeared.[13]

FORREST COUNTY CONSTABLE CHASES UFOs THROUGH TWO COUNTIES

In October 1973, a Forrest County Constable responded to a call from a resident in Petal, Mississippi, about bright strange lights seen overhead. He said by the time he arrived at the address:

> When I got there, I spotted it up over the Petal High School. It looked like an old-time wind up top with yellow lights all around it.

He said he followed it for about 30 miles through Forrest and Jones Counties, hoping to see it land so he could see if anybody got out.

> I followed it up to the Jones-Forrest County line. It slowed down over a field and some lights came out the side. They looked sort of like blow torches. Then it went back up north. I followed it five miles and it went toward the Tallahalla Swamp. I got pretty close to it when my car died. It was just like someone had cut the motor off. In about fifteen minutes, my car started up again like nothing was wrong. Sheriff deputies had tried to contact me by radio, but everything was dead during that time.

He said he chased the object through forests and swamps through the two counties and he lost it when it did a double flip and then just disappeared.[14]

GLOWING UFO TERRIFIES POLICE AND CIVILIANS

On July 8, 1974, over Ravenna, Italy, at 11:15 p.m., a UFO was spotted by a toll collector while at work in his booth. He saw a saucer-

shaped object with glowing multi-colored lights gliding silently across the sky. At the same time a man, his wife, and some friends in a car on the same turnpike witnessed it also. They described it as saucer shaped, hovering and glowing. One of the witnesses described it as looking "like a French beret with a yellow center-like halo. We were all scared to death."

The driver pulled over to a roadside phone and called the police. The chief of police went out to meet with the witnesses. As they were talking, the object appeared.

"It looked like a discus with an orange light underneath and a blue light on top," the officer said.

At that moment, the head of the highway patrol was driving in his car and happened to look up into the sky. He said, "I saw something round shoot up into the sky, turning from blue to red to orange. I was absolutely flabbergasted."

The next day a farm worker reported seeing the object land in a field nearby and then rises again. The chief of police officer went out to the area with some men and found circular scorch marks on the ground about twenty yards wide.

Three nights later, about 125 miles northeast of Ravenna, a similar object was seen landing and taking off. A traffic cop witnessed the object from his home with his family. He said that when it took off, there was a smell of sulphur. The next morning, the fire chief went out to the field to inspect the grounds and found scorch marks over 400 square yards. The marks were all 20-yard-wide circles on the ground. [15]

KINGSTON, NEW YORK

July 8, 1974

A large ellipsoidal UFO was spotted over a ballpark by two police officers at 1 a.m. It responded to a signal from the police car spotlight by shining a light on the car and the officers. [16]

LACONIA, NEW HAMPSHIRE

August 12, 1974

While out on routine patrol, two police officers in Laconia, New Hampshire, witnessed a UFO. They immediately radioed the dispatcher what they were seeing, and turned on a tape recorder in the patrol car to record the events as they happened. They then tried to signal the object with their emergency lights. What occurred then became an experience that neither officer will ever forget.

When they turned on their emergency lights, the object sent a beam of light down in response. Each time the car lights flashed, the object changed colors. It then began to move closer to them. "We estimated that the UFO came within 450 to 500 yards of us when we flashed our lights," one officer said. "It scared the living tar out of me. I felt in danger of my life and I guess I panicked. I shouted at my partner to turn off our lights and the craft backed off," he added. They described the object as shaped like a football.

Within minutes of reporting this object, two other officers arrived, one from the Belknap County Sheriff's office and the other from the Belmont Police Department. While they were watching, two other UFOs joined the first one. The officers watched the objects move closer to them, then soar up and then down. The objects backed away, then hovered for a while before moving off out of sight.

The following are some excerpts from the recording made by the two officers in their patrol car:

Dispatcher:
Can you see any outline of the object at all?

Officer 1:
Yeah, we both thought we saw a saucer outline of some kind. I think the object dived and rose several times. Now it is responding to signals.

Officer 2:
Tell 'em we flashed lights at it and it seemed to flash lights back.

Officer 1:
We see blue and red lights on the rear end of it. The lights are very good, continually get pretty bright and then dull out. When we flick our lights, it responds, changing colors. I don't know about you, but I'm nervous as hell.

Officer 2:
Let's see if it will signal us some more.

Officers 1:
Look at him. See him change? Change to blue!

Officer2:
Is he coming? He is getting closer!

Dispatcher:
Be careful! Don't get too close.

(In a very panicky voice, Officer 1 shouted at Officer 2 to turn off the patrol car's emergency lights)

Officer 1:
Hold it! Hold it! Hold it! Hold it! See him move now? See him move over? Look at him! See the outline? See him? He's coming at us! Look at him dive.

Officer 2:
You see any lights over the trees?

Officer 1:
I saw one beam go down.

Officer 2:
Yeah, that's what I saw too. Tell 'em we seem to see a beam from time to time coming from it.

Officer 1:
I saw the outline.

Officer 2:
Like it was a football-shaped thing.

Officer 1:
Look at it now. Look at it move. Looks like it's getting closer.

Officer 2:
It is. Look at it go! Look at him!

Officer 1:
Hit your blues.

Officer 2:
Look at it move!

Officer 1:
He is definitely responding to our signal.
(**To dispatcher**): Be advised this thing is signaling us.
(**To officer 2**): Look at it move. See him? See him? See him signal back? I don't know about you, Mark, but I'm bum excited about all this.

Officer 2:
I think it's neat.

Officer 1:
You know what's going to happen, though. When we tell all of this to the others, we're going to be called a bunch of lunatics.

Officer 2:
Not if we get them to come up here and look at it.

Officer 1:
Yeah, they'll probably say it's a star.

Sheriff's Deputy:
(*Who was driving toward the scene*):
Be advised that I have the object in sight. It's quite a ways off now but I can see the blue lights and the red lights at times and it is moving – and now I can see yellow lights.

Officer 1:
See the red, see? Red and blue? See the lights? Look at 'em, look at 'em, see the lights? See the red and red? There's blue, there's everything.

Dispatcher:
The Franklin cruiser, (*a patrol car from the nearby town of Franklin, NH*) advises that he can see three of them [UFOs], so you're not alone in reporting the sightings in this area.

Officer1:
Thank God for that.

The tape ended at this time.[17]

Dazzling Formation of UFOs Puts
on Aerial Display Over Nebraska

August 15, 1974, in various parts of Nebraska, UFOs were witnessed by a number of police officers, citizens, and even the mayor of one town. In Newman Grove, twenty UFOs were seen in the sky, glowing in brilliant colors and darting up and down and sideways for three nights straight. The local police chief and about twenty of the townspeople went out into a field to watch these objects.

The mayor reported, "I saw sparkling bright colored lights. I watched them for about twenty minutes each night. I never saw such things before in my life."

The objects were described as oblong with little bumps on top. There were as many as twenty UFOs hovering in a triangle. Blinking lights in red, green, and white surrounded the objects.

Ninety miles away in the town of Crete, a police officer stopped his patrol car when he first spotted the objects. "I jumped out of the car and grabbed my binoculars for a better look at the dozen or so pulsating lights. They were whirling around very high in the sky. I've studied astronomy as a hobby since I was a kid, so I know stars when I see them and these weren't stars. I didn't hesitate to report these UFOs to my chief," the officer said. He also said the police radio picked up two other policemen twenty miles away and they sounded frantic. He described the objects as brightly lit with lumps on the top. The first night they were stationary for about two hours.

"Suddenly, and with a tremendous burst of speed, they silently darted straight up. Then they dropped back and shot sideways, never losing their triangular formation," he said.

Nearby, a Saline County deputy sheriff was watching a UFO with red, green, and white colored lights all contained in what looked like a tight sparkling circle. Soon he spotted three more just like the first and then there were more and more. He got on his radio and the dispatcher told him that other police officers were watching them in the sky in other nearby towns.[18]

Altamont, New York

August 19, 1974

Two women, a director, and an employee of an Altamont, New York nursing home, witnessed a UFO. One of the women reported the incident to her son, a State Police investigator. The description was very similar to the same one reported by the State Police on August 20, 1974.[19]

0 0 0

Jim received an email from someone who introduced himself as the grandson of the above-mentioned trooper. We connected by phone and he gave me some more information that he had learned from his grandfather. The trooper had seen the UFO that evening while he was out on patrol, before getting the call from another witness. When he saw it, he stopped along a quiet rural road and got out of his car. He first heard a buzzing noise, thought it was his radio, so he looked into the car to see if there was a call, then a very bright beam of light shone down on him briefly. When it turned off, the object sped off quickly with no noise other than a "phtt" sound. Then he got the call to respond to Berne New York to see a woman about another sighting. She said a UFO was flying above her property near her barn for a while before it left. She heard no noise at all from the object.

SIX ASTONISHED AIR TRAFFIC CONTROLLERS TRACK UFO ON RADAR – AT 3600 MILES AN HOUR

About 8 p.m., on August 20, 1974, a UFO was seen by residents who reported it to the State Police near Round Lake, New York, about twelve miles north of Albany. The police were able to see the object and notified the air traffic control tower at the Albany Airport to see if they had anything on radar. The men in the tower were amazed to see the object show up on their radar screen.

One of the air traffic controllers recalled:

> We've received all kinds of UFO reports here over the years, but this is the only time we were able to detect anything in the radar screens. It was just an amazing experience. We were as mystified as the police as to what was up there. It was uncanny that policemen were watching what seemed to be the same object that appeared as a blip on our radar screen. I watched as it split into two separate targets. Later, it split into as many as four. About an hour after we'd begun watching these objects, I contacted an Air Force pilot on a training flight about twenty miles north of Albany. He reported he could see some lights in the south which were stationary. Shortly after that, he suddenly reported seeing an object that moved across his path from north to south on a blaze of orange light – traveling so fast he was shouting with excitement on the radio. I picked up the object on radar south of the military aircraft and coming toward the airport at an estimated 3,600 miles per hour. When it got to the airport, it vanished.

Another air controller stated:

It came straight for the airport at an unbelievable speed. I was watching my radar screen and just couldn't believe my eyes. There was no explanation for what happened next. The object seemed to be heading right for the control tower. But once it seemed to get above us it just vanished.

A third air traffic controller stated:

The military pilot was really excited. He said he'd never seen anything move so quickly in his life – and neither have I!

The control tower supervisor said:

The objects were visible on all four radar screens and we observed them for more than two hours.

One of the state troopers said:

I just couldn't believe my eyes. I saw one object hovering in the sky. Then I saw another come out of the north at a hell of a speed. It was red or orange. And it flashed right overhead. I don't know of any aircraft that could travel that fast, and it sure wasn't a meteor.

Another trooper said:

I saw three or four objects moving at height between 500 and 1500 feet. At times they moved slowly and at other times they were real fast. It was strange. I've never seen anything like it.[20]

GLOWING METALLIC UFO ASTONISHES POLICE AND SCORES OF TOWNSPEOPLE

On September 15, 1974, at 10:30 p.m., a patrolman from Vale, Oregon, saw a metallic-looking object with bright multi-colored lights hovering, moving up and down, and moving at incredible speeds through the sky. From the 15th until the 20th, the object was seen by at least seven police officers and scores of citizens over the communities of Vale, Ontario, and Nyssa, Oregon.

The object was described as disc shaped with yellow, blue, green, and red pulsating lights. No sound was heard from the object. It was reported at one point by the officer as being 1,000 feet above the ground and as big as a house.

Suddenly, it shot up another couple of thousand feet, stopping dead in its tracks. Then it dropped back to its original position. Suddenly it moved again, shooting off toward the south covering maybe 30 miles in just a few seconds.

Two nights later, on the 17th, a deputy sheriff and two patrolmen saw the object at 2 a.m. from different patrol cars. Over the next few nights, many others saw the object moving at incredible speeds across the sky. [21]

UFO CHANGES COLOR, SIZE, AND SHAPE DURING EERIE AERIAL SHOW OVER NORTH CAROLINA

On February 26, 1975, a police officer watched a UFO along with several residents of Durham, North Carolina between the hours of 1:30 a.m. and 3:30 a.m.

According to a dispatcher's taped recording of the police officer, he said:

I can see it. I don't know what it is. It's sitting perfectly still. It gets bigger and then smaller and it changes shape. It sits there and then it moves, it's real weird.

In an interview with the *National Enquirer,* he stated:

The UFO scared the hell out of me. There was an awesome sense of power as it moved across the sky, secure in knowing that there was nothing we can do. I had a feeling of complete helplessness.

He later commented:

After about a half an hour, the most amazing thing happened. Before my very eyes, it actually started to change shape. It grew longer and longer until thirty seconds later it became three times its original length. It was hanging there motionless like a giant chocolate éclair. It held this shape for about thirty minutes, and then it slowly shrank back again to its original smaller, circular shape. Suddenly it shot to the left with great speed, parallel to the earth for about a half mile. Then it shot back to the right to its original position.

About thirty officers from all over the area had seen the UFO. The Chief of Communications officer for Durham Police Department stated:

> There were UFO reports from Durham, Raleigh, and Chapel Hill, as well as the North Carolina Highway Patrol.

He also added:

> A strange thing happened as the UFO moved over Durham County. The high band communications channel used by the Sheriff's Department was jammed. For five minutes all we heard was a high-pitched hum. We never picked up that sound on that channel before or since the UFO." [22]

GLOWING UFO BAFFLES MORE THAN 30 POLICE OFFICERS FOR 4 DAYS

As UFOs appeared over Durham, North Carolina, more sightings continued in other parts of the state. Between April 3 and April 6, more than thirty police officers witnessed brightly colored lights from an object flying, hovering, and landing.

A Lumberton County Sheriff's radio dispatcher reported that calls started coming in after 1 a.m. on the morning of April 3rd. He said, "We were swamped with calls from the public and thirty officers reported seeing a strange object."

"I saw the object hovering about fifty feet over the town's water tank," replied one officer in response to a call from a citizen who reported the object.

The officer described the object:

> It seemed to be triangular or *V* shaped. I could make out reddish lights on one side of it and blue and green lights on the other. I thought it was about the size of a Cadillac. The strange thing is that there was no sound at all. It appeared to have a solid hull and one big spotlight.

As the officer watched the object, it just shot away at breathtaking speed. "I heard on my patrol car radio that it was spotted over St. Pauls, fifteen miles away – just ninety seconds later," he added.

In St. Pauls, a police officer and a security guard gave chase to the UFO, after they had spotted a red flash "like an explosion."

The security guard said, "We took off after it, but lost it. Then we stopped the car and just waited." He said that the UFO seemed to just come out of nowhere. "There is was again… It seemed to be triangular, maybe *V* shaped, with blue lights all around the edges and a pulsating ball of red light in the center. There were two big beams like searchlights… The next thing I knew, it took off at terrific speed – without a sound."

A Hoke County Deputy Sheriff next saw the UFO. "It seemed to be traveling about the speed of a jet, but far closer to the ground than I've ever seen a jet fly."

On April 5th, the Lumberton radio dispatcher looked toward the sky on his way home after his shift and saw the object. He said that it had appeared less than 200 feet above his car and it flashed its lights in response to him flashing his car lights at it. It then moved off at a terrific speed and vanished.

The next day at dawn, a White Lakes, North Carolina police chief witnessed a similar triangular-shaped object with a pulsating red light.

The next day, on the 6th of April, a State Police Officer reported seeing a similar shaped object during the early morning hours.

Later that day, about 5:15 p.m., an off-duty Robeson County Deputy Sheriff, while returning home from an outing with his family, spotted the UFO directly over the road ahead of them. They watched the UFO as it made a sweeping dive toward a field 10 yards away.

"I slowed down and my wife let out a gasp because she thought it was going to hit a farmhouse," he said. "But the thing just disappeared behind the farmhouse without a sound."[23]

HUGE GLOWING UFO HOVERS OVER HIGH TENSION TOWER AND FOLLOWS POLICE SPOTLIGHT

In the early morning hours of November 4, 1975, two UFOs were seen glowing red and green as they flew in around 3:45 a.m. coming inland from Lake Erie, by two patrolmen, a police dispatcher, and a tow truck operator in Madison, Ohio.

"It was incredible," one officer said. "They were in formation and then they broke off. One hovered over Madison and the other headed northeast."

The object hovering over Madison, Ohio, seemed to have a great deal of interest for a high tension tower.

One officer reported,

The one near the tower leveled off and slowly approached as though it was maneuvering carefully as if it was trying to get as close to the tower as possible. When it got directly over the tower, the reddish green light faded and the object began to glow pure white, so bright I couldn't see if it was actually touching the tower.

He added:

I was about a half a mile away and I couldn't estimate how large it was. When I held up my hand at arm's length to judge its size, it was larger than my hand. It was huge.

Just as the white light reached its peak, the object streaked off across the sky so fast you couldn't see it move. Then it approached again, glowing red. It made about twenty passes at the tower, each time approaching the same way, and then zipping off into the darkness.

The other officer stated,:

It was an eerie feeling. It was as though someone or something was watching us, checking us out.

He also said that the UFO reacted to his turning the patrol car spot light on and off.

The first time I put the spotlight on, the object moved away. Then I flicked it on and off a few more times – and the object started to move toward the spotlight.

The two officers said they watched this object flying to and from the tower for about ninety minutes, as if it was attracted to it.

It was astonishing! It seemed to be intrigued by the light. I didn't know what to do – so I turned the light off real quick.

The officer decided to go and investigate the other UFO.

As I left the area, the object moved along above my car for a while and for some mysterious reason, my radio wouldn't work.

He came across an auto wrecker who reported his two-way radio wasn't working either.

A police dispatcher working during the time of the sightings said that they had received at least a dozen calls about the object.

> I could see it from my window once, and I went outside to see it, but I got scared and didn't go out again.[24]

N.J. PATROLMAN: ENORMOUS, BRILLIANT UFO SHOT IN FROM OCEAN – SO CLOSE, IT COULD HAVE SWALLOWED ME UP

At 5:15 a.m., on January, 20 1976, a patrolman from Ventnor, New Jersey, in the company of a newspaper reporter, observed a UFO from the shores of Atlantic City. The officer was giving the reporter a ride home when they spotted an object about a mile off shore that was so huge that it seemed to fill the whole windshield.

Curious, the patrolman drove his car out onto the beach to see it. "All of a sudden, the object came straight in toward us," he said. "I immediately backed my car up a ramp and off the beach. I've never seen anything like this before. It came in very, very close, just over the breakers, about 500 feet from the car. It was so huge it seemed to fill in the whole windshield. I couldn't see anything else. It had a very bright white light in its center with a yellow haze around it twice the size of the light. When it got close, you could see three small reddish-orange points in it, in the shape of a triangle."

The patrolman radioed the Atlantic City Police Department and requested some officers to come out to them and witness what they were seeing. About twenty policemen responded and saw the object shortly before it vanished.

One officer said, "The light seemed to get dimmer and then brighter as we watched. We checked for helicopters, but there weren't any up that night."

Another officer said, "It appeared to be a glowing light out over the ocean. As I gazed at it, suddenly it just disappeared in front of my eyes. I was shocked."[25]

MYSTERIOUS UFOs TRAIL TERRIFIED WOMEN IN CAR

Two women driving home from an outing in Gadsden, Alabama, the night of February 18, 1976, saw a mysterious light about 8 p.m. to their left in a nearby wooded area. The driver, a 33-year Sunday school teacher, and her passenger, first saw a single large, orange object. Then four more lights, similar to the first one, appeared. The five lights followed the car for many miles, first alongside the car and then trailing behind it.

Eight days later, on the 26th of February, an Alabama State Police Officer saw similar objects to the ones seen by the two women.

> I saw six or eight on the night of the 26th. They were just round balls of light – some orange, some white, and some pure red. One of them stopped in the air and went up and down like a yo-yo.

Two other officers from Attalla saw the same objects the same night. One said:

> My partner and I saw three red objects speeding toward the southwest.

An assistant police chief of Sardis reported:

> I saw an orange ball of fire come across the sky at high speed.

Another police officer from Boaz, just northwest of Gadsden reported:

> I saw a real bright orange ball streak across the sky.

A deputy sheriff from Guntersville, Alabama, said he saw a bluish green UFO during the night of March 14th.

While driving with an auxiliary police officer, patrolman from Rainbow City said he saw one on the night of March 28th. "It was a large yellowish fiery ball," he said.[26]

TERRIFYING UFO ATTACK KNOCKS POLICEMAN UNCONSCIOUS, IMMOBILIZES HIS CAR, AND BLANKS OUT TELEVISION SETS IN THE AREA

On the night of April 3, 1976, at 11 p.m., a former police chief working as a relief officer saw an orange glow at the top of a hill. Thinking it was a fire, he went to investigate it.

0 0 0

When I arrived, I saw this huge object, as high as a two-story house and about 250 feet across. It was silver in color and had an extremely bright orange light at the top, so bright I couldn't look straight at it. Suddenly, the craft rose and a blue flash of light shot out.

At this time, the car's lights and radio went dead. I don't remember any more until somebody was asking me if I needed help.

The police officer spent the next fourteen days in the hospital recovering from its effects. The officer was a thirty-year veteran of the police force and a former World War II combat fighter pilot, not one to buckle under the slightest pressure. [27]

MAHOPAC, NEW YORK

April 1976
Three police officers and about twenty residents watched an object in the sky, spinning in a clockwise direction. According to one police officer, who had been summoned by a resident watching the object, it was round and emitted colors which changed from red to yellow to blue. Another police officer described the light as having a strobe effect. The sighting occurred at 9:30 p.m. and lasted for about a half hour.[28]

MAHOPAC, NEW YORK

June 1976
In the evening, two local policemen spotted a spinning round object "emitting three different colors." One officer said that it looked like a light in the sky with a strobe effect.[29]

ALTAMONT, NEW YORK

February 8, 1977
At 9:30 p.m., four members of the Albany County Sheriff's Department observed an object hovering in the sky. They estimated it to be saucer shaped and about forty feet across and twenty feet high. There were lights all around the center of the object and various colored lights flashed. No sound was heard and they estimated the object to be about half a mile away. The object was first seen as orange in color, then turned to gray.[30]

FLORENCE, KENTUCKY

January 19, 1978

Two patrolmen from the Erlanger Police Department were on their way home at 9:30 p.m., after their duty shift, when one of them caught a glimpse of a light in the sky. When he looked at it closely, he saw an egg-shaped object that was lime green with sparkling white lights. The witness told the other officer, who was driving, to look out the window, but he looked in the wrong direction and didn't see the object.

At the same time, not too far away, the witnessing patrolman's niece and son were playing in the snow when a brilliant green light flashed in the sky about sixty feet over them. The young boy began to get scared and started to cry. The niece went into the house with him. Her grandmother said that she looked as white as a ghost. When the patrolman arrived home, he called the Cincinnati Airport Tower, and the man at the tower laughed at him and told him he had only seen an airplane. The patrolman said that if it was an airplane flying that fast and that low, they would have a big crash on their hands. He also said that the object was too erratic to be an airplane. The patrolman advised that if you can picture a clock, it started at 3 o'clock and went over to 9 o'clock, then shot up to 12 o'clock and dropped straight down to 6 o'clock.[31]

SALAMANCA, NEW YORK

March 19, 1978

At least three different sightings of UFOs with multi-colored lights were reported to the police in Cattaraugus County. Several individuals, including officers in the Cattaraugus Sheriff's Department and the Salamanca Police Department, reported seeing the objects between 11:40 p.m., Sunday, and 12:45 a.m., Monday. A Salamanca patrolman said that one of the objects was triangular and looked sort of like a boomerang. He said the object displayed a series of changing blue, red, green and white lights.[32]

SYRACUSE, NEW YORK

March 29, 1978

At about 9:15 p.m., a city police officer was dispatched to Kramer Street in response to an urgent call of a UFO sighting. The officer and several residents watched a diamond-shaped object with a crisscross series of red, blue, and green lights. The police officer called for a helicopter

to respond to the location, and as the helicopter approached, the object quickly shot up into the air and disappeared. The police report stated that the helicopter crew did not see the object, but a witness on the scene stated that when she asked if any of the crew had seen anything, she was told unofficially that they did.[33]

BALDWINSVILLE, NEW YORK

April 6, 1978

At about 10:05 p.m., a police officer and his family observed an object that appeared over some woods adjacent to his property. The object had a narrow band of red, blue, green, and yellow lights running around the middle, and emitted bright flashes of light. It moved back and forth and, at certain points, ascended slightly. About ten minutes later, two extreme flashes of light arced to the ground from the object, and the lights in the witness's home and those of some 3,000 other residents in the Jordan-Elbridge area went out. A police helicopter was sent out to investigate the sighting and the occupants witnessed the flashes. The witnesses stated that as the helicopter approached, the object accelerated rapidly and flew away. The Hancock Airport radar operators picked up a UFO on their screens at the same time and location, and confirmed this sighting.[34]

WARREN, MINNESOTA

August 27, 1979

While out on routine patrol, Deputy Sheriff Val Johnson observed a light in a field off into the distance along the highway. The officer drove toward the light to see what it was. As he approached it, the light seemed to suddenly zoom toward his vehicle and blinded the officer temporarily. The light, or something, hit his vehicle. The car ended up about 950 feet further down the road leaving tire marks along the way. Val Johnson had lost consciousness and when regaining it, he radioed to dispatch for assistance.

An investigation of the accident was conducted. It showed that the car suffered some strange damage. The inside light of a double front headlight on the driver's side was smashed. The outside light suffered no damage at all. There was a small round dent on the front hood and the windshield had severe damage. On the roof of the patrol car was a small hole in one of the warning lights and both antennae on the roof

were bent. The remains of small bugs ("BUG TAR") that covered the antennae where the bends were, was stretched around the bend but not otherwise disturbed. This indicates that there was no direct contact of a bending force with the surface of the antennas. Thus, they were not bent by someone grabbing the antennas and applying force.

Officer Johnson recalled losing consciousness and, after awakening and calling the police station to report the incident, he discovered that his personal watch and the car clock were both about fourteen minutes slow, as if they had been stopped for about fourteen minutes.

The investigation could come up with no cause for the accident. There was no sign of hitting another vehicle, no low flying planes and it was determined that Officer Johnson did not hoax this incident.[35]

HUDSON VALLEY, NEW YORK

During the period of 1982 till about 1985, in the area known as the Hudson Valley section of New York State and parts of western Connecticut, a rash of sightings stirred up a lot of fear and excitement. When the Yorktown Police Department in New York was receiving a lot of reports of sightings, one report was unique in that it came from one of their own officers. His first reaction when he saw the object over the middle of town was that it was a jetliner in trouble. However, he immediately realized that it couldn't be a jetliner because he watched it turn around in a 180 degrees direction and then slowly drift away. No jetliner can move in that way, but what the object was is still a mystery.

Around 9 p.m., on March 24, 1983, residents in the New Castle area started calling the New Castle Police Department, reporting sightings of an unusual object looking like a string of white lights making a half circle. The dispatcher sent out a patrolman to look into the sightings. At the same time, another New Castle police officer, Andy Sadoff, a policewoman with five years on the job, was watching an object come over a hill while sitting in her patrol car along a highway, on the lookout for speeders.

> All of a sudden from over a hill, I saw a string of while lights, very large, forming a half circle. It was just coming over the ridge and it caught my attention because it was so large. It then turned left and started coming around to where I was parked. I started shaking my head thinking that this was strange because it made no sound and it was large. It then passed over my vehicle and headed toward the town.
>
> Then about four minutes later, it came back in my direction. It turned toward my car once again, but this time, it was much lower. The way the object moved was very smooth, as if it were gliding. When it

came around, I could see the shape better. It was in the shape of a *V* with white lights on the top and green lights on the bottom.

It was heading toward me and flying right for my car, so I looked out the window and did the normal thing. I locked the doors. This time it was very low. I stuck my head out the window and it stopped right over my car. It then hovered there about twenty seconds and I could see a mass that was very large. Behind it – behind the lights, that is – I could see a large solid object.

She then got on the radio and called other officers who claimed that they were also getting many calls on the object. The entire sighting, she said, lasted about eight minutes and then it just drifted slowly over the ridge and disappeared.

When asked to estimate how big it might have been she said:

If I held my arms apart two feet, I would just be able to fit in the object. I estimated its size at about 300 feet from end to end.[36]

STILLWATER, NEW YORK

October 7, 1994

A high school girl opened her back door to let a cat inside when she noticed lights in the sky over a field behind her back yard. The lights were red and green and were moving in a circular motion around a saucer-shaped object. She was also able to see an occasional yellow light. There was a little white light beneath it, but not part of the object. She said the white light resembled a star. As she watched the object, a second object moved in and hovered next to the first one, but the second one seemed to be on its side. The second object began to move around the first. Soon, three more objects approached them and formed a circular pattern. They stayed like this for about five to ten minutes, until the three new ones moved to another portion of the sky and formed a triangle. There were, altogether, about ten witnesses, including a police sergeant from Stillwater. When asked what he thought about the sightings, he said that he didn't know what it could have been, but he was certain that they weren't stars. The investigation revealed that there were about thirty witnesses altogether from various towns nearby, who all apparently saw the same thing.

Originally, witnesses reported twelve UFOs hovering over the witness's home at one time. Later investigations proved that at least some of them were stars. The ones that moved, however, were clearly not stars, and remain unidentified.[37]

LAGRANGE, GEORGIA

March 1997

In March 1997, a retired police chief and his daughter were out in their yard when they both saw two objects in the sky that were identical in shape and size. Each looked like a white car fuse, both nose to nose in an inverted *V* as though one were charging the other. The police chief called to his wife to come outside and bring the camera. As she ran out of the house and into the yard, he said that one of the UFOs "took off like a bullet." The remaining UFO began to move slowly, then picked up speed.

With only one shot left in the camera, the wife snapped a picture of the UFO. On later examination of this photo, a dim vertical line is visible down the center of the object.

The police chief has been an officer for thirty-five years, fifteen of which he has served as Chief. He stated:

> Frank, I used to laugh at people who reported UFOs. I'm not laughing any more. These things are real. I don't know where they come from, but one thing I do know, is they ain't ours.

The object in his photo is identical to the object seen and videotaped over Ticonderoga, New York, and which is referred to as the Flying Peanut later in this book.

SCHENECTADY, NEW YORK

September 23, 1998

At about 4:50 a.m., while going to work, a Schenectady police officer with eight years of service, noticed a green-white orb traveling southeast through the sky. It was twice as bright as the North Star and completely soundless. He described it as traveling half as fast as a shooting star, much faster than he ever saw an airplane travel. He looked carefully and saw no other navigational or strobe lights on it.[38]

ST. CLAIR COUNTY, OHIO

January 5, 2000

On January 5th of 2000, a police officer (who wishes to remain anonymous) with the Lebanon Police Department responding to a civilian witness report of unexplained lights, himself observing two brilliant

0 0 0

white lights in the sky as he was approaching the area. He moved toward the lights at a faster speed, and the lights appeared on his left side of the patrol car and then on the right side. He began to think that this might be an airplane in trouble so he turned on his overhead flashing lights, stopped his car, and turned off the radio so he could listen for noise. There was none.

He could now see that the object was massive, shaped like a narrow triangle. It was not moving very fast nor was it moving very slow. He estimated the size to be about 75 feet in length and about 40 feet in width at each of the corners. It appeared to be about 100 feet away from him, and about 1,000 feet in elevation. The object had three bright white lights, one at each corner, and one smaller flashing red light near the two rear white lights. He watched as the object pivoted in mid-air and turned from a Southerly direction to a Southwesterly direction, then slowly started to move away. The officer got in his car and radioed to headquarters what he was watching. It began to pick up speed, and he watched as it moved very quickly towards the town of Shiloh.

A police officer with the Shiloh Police Department radioed that he could see the object, and reported that he could see three brilliant white lights shining down from it. However, he said that the lights did not illuminate the ground below. He estimated the object to be about 100 feet in altitude and about 75 to 100 yards wide. He rolled down his window to listen for any noise but could not hear anything. He decided to pull over and get out of the car to observe better, and the object increased its speed and disappeared in a Westerly direction. He estimated that the object, when he first observed it, was moving about 15 MPH and increased its speed to about 80 – 100 MPH.[39]

LAKE COUNTY, OHIO

June 16, 2004

On Wednesday, June 16, 2004, a deputy sheriff in Lake County, Ohio, witnessed an unusual object. Lake County is located near Cleveland, along Lake Erie.

The deputy was off-duty, and outside at about 5:45 p.m. He was looking at the sky for weather conditions when he first noticed a plane in the sky, then another object somewhat higher and behind the plane. He could tell that this other object was not a plane, as it was moving much faster and also had a triangular shape, with no wings or tail. The sighting lasted only about 15 to 20 seconds and then the object was gone.

The next day, he had forgotten about the object until his wife had mentioned having seen a strange object in the sky at the same time.

She described it as triangular in shape, dark gray, and without lights or markings. The object had frightened her because while she was watching it, she felt it was watching her also. It had stopped and hovered silently about 100 feet above a tree. The officer then told her of his own sighting.[40]

STEPHANVILLE, TEXAS

January 8, 2008

On January 8, 2008, an Erath County deputy sheriff was outside when he spotted a UFO overhead. He had his eight-year-old son with him. Neither spoke about the UFO to anybody until they heard other people talking about it. A local newspaper quoted him:

> I was outside with my eight-year-old son, Ryan, when I saw lights. It was like nothing I've ever seen before. It was dark already. At first it was two red burning glows that went away and then came back on. I went inside to tell my wife. When I came back out I saw something like lights you'd see in a bar. My little boy and I counted and we came up with nine flashes and they were real spread out. But I couldn't see them attached to anything, just the lights.
>
> So I went to my pickup and got my binoculars to see if I could see a plane or something. Even with the binoculars there was no outline. It started moving towards Stephenville and moving so fast I had trouble following it with my binoculars. It covered a big area. It sounds crazy but we really saw what we saw. As a matter of fact, I mentioned it to an officer in Stephenville and he called me up and said to get the Stephenville paper because I wasn't going to believe what was in it. I also went to the Dublin paper but they had no other reports on it so I just dropped it. But my little boy went to school the next day and told everybody all about what we'd seen.[41]

When asked about this, a U.S. Air Force official said that it was reflections off two commercial airplanes and that they had no jets in the sky. A week later they claimed that they had made a mistake about the previous report and that they had been running a training session and had five F-16s in the sky at the time. What the Air Force had not been able to explain was why most of the witnesses reported that they had seen these objects hovering and not just flying. The witnesses also stated that they had heard no sound.[42]

UFO REPORTS
FROM AROUND THE WORLD

AWESOME FORMATION OF UFOS OVER JAPAN
ASTONISHES POLICE AND GOVERNMENT OFFICIALS

Many UFOs were sighted in cities traveling north to south, covering well over 700 miles in less than an hour. At least fifteen to twenty objects were seen moving in a straight formation inside a misty cloud on January 15, 1975.

Hundreds of frantic callers phoned into the various police stations and governmental installations throughout Japan. The police station in Asahikawa, Japan, a city in the northern island of Hokkaido, received the first call at about 5:15 p.m. One officer said:

> All of the callers reported seeing a huge cloud passing over the city. They said they saw orange objects inside the cloud, moving in a straight line.

As the UFOs passed over the city of Morioka, on the main island of Japan, the police chief and a few other police officers stepped outside to see what all of the excited phone calls were about. The chief said:

> We were astonished by what we saw. There was a huge, misty white cloud, perhaps a third of a mile across, soaring across the sky; and inside this cloud were about twenty separate orange lights, all in a row. Each of the lights trailed a small gray tail. The strange thing was the total silence. They were in sight for about thirty seconds, then, they accelerated at high speeds.

In the city of Iwaki, Japan, the local police chief and two other police officers also went outside their station to get a look at what was being reported. The police chief said:

> I was amazed. In the sky, heading from north to south, directly over the city, was this enormous, transparent white cloud. Within the mist I could see about twenty luminous objects. I'd guess the glowing objects were about 20 to 30 feet wide. They looked like they were flying at 200 miles per hour at 10,000 feet, but they quickly gained speed and vanished.

At the same time calls were pouring into the various police stations, calls were also being made to government weather installations. All replied that they had nothing showing up on radar and nothing could be seen in the sky, except at the Tokyo International Airport. There, one observer who saw the objects stated:

> I was mystified. Nothing showed up on my radar. I reported my sighting to the airport control tower and they told me nothing showed up on their radar either.[43]

PRUFOS

While browsing the Internet, we came across a website that was new to us, though I thought I had seen everything relating to UFOs. The name of this site was Police Reporting UFO Sightings (PRUFOS). It is a collection of police-witnessed UFO sightings, primarily from England. The PRUFOS site was founded in November 2001 by Gary Heseltine, an officer with the British Transport Police, and a Detective Constable with a wide range of experience of criminal investigations. While the database is mostly concerned with British reports, it also includes many reports from around the world including the United States.

Heseltine's interest into the field of Ufology began in 1975, when he experienced his first sighting at the age of fifteen. At the time, he was in Bottesford, Scunthrope, in the county of Lincolnshire. In his words:

> As I walked along a foot path adjacent to my comprehensive school (Frederick Gough Comprehensive) I saw a brilliant white light pass from my right to my left. As the object moved slowly across the landscape, all electrical power behind its flight path cut off, plunging the area into darkness. As I continued to watch it, a series of further power cuts followed. My then girlfriend was with me at the time and

also observed the object. Because it was heading in the direction of my home, I decided to drop her off first and then race back on my cycle in an effort to get ahead of it by way of a short cut. This I did and just made it in time to observe it pass over the garden of my home. Having gotten home, I rushed inside and told my parents that I believed a power cut was imminent, but they only looked at me, bemused. As soon as it had passed over, a thirty-minute power cut followed. The UFO was seen against a backdrop of a clear summer's night sky and appeared to have no sound.

We are presenting the following reports with the permission of Mr. Haseltine. Sightings in the PRUFOS database are listed in many categories such as Police-Related UFO Investigations, On-Duty Police Sightings, Off-Duty Police Sightings, Pre-Police Sightings, Post-Police Sightings, Worldwide Police Sightings, exhibits in which drawings are displayed, and so on. Some examples of the postings follow.

ON-DUTY POLICE SIGHTINGS

1950

GOWERTON, WALES

Monday, February 11, 1950
Following a report by a member of the public of two UFOs in the skies above Gowerton, Detective Sergeant Ambose Davies observed a single white ball of flame. It was much brighter than any star and after a few seconds the object divided into two. The officer then stated that following their separation from each other, there appeared to be some kind of tether between them. The officer rules out any aircraft of natural phenomena.[44]

Source – *UFO Magazine* Press Archives

CHICHESTER NEAR BOGNOR REGIS

0600 hours
Following a report by a member of the public, two uniform officers, observed a strange object in the sky above Chichester. At the same time, in Bognor Regis, just seven miles away, a third police officer also saw the

object in the sky. He described it as a "tadpole-shaped" object. He went on to state that the object had "lit" up Bognor. [45]

1966

Wilmslow, Cheshire

0410 hours in March (exact date not posted)
A uniformed officer in Wilmslow, Cheshire, observed a thirty-foot UFO flying at an altitude of only 30 feet and at a distance of 100 yards from his position.

1967

Stoney Cross, New Forest

May 7, 1967 at 0130 hours
On 05/07/1967 at 0130 hours, in Stoney Cross, New Forest, a uniformed officer was dispatched to follow up on a report of an orange ball-shaped UFO by a member of the public. He was able to corroborate the sighting of the orange UFO that he said did a "loop the loop" before heading away.

Gosport

October 1967
In October of 1967 in Gosport, two uniformed officers observed a red and white colored UFO while on mobile patrol in the Little Anglesey Road area. The UFO was seen above the submarine base at HMS *Dolphin*. They observed the UFO for five minutes.

Between Okehampton and Holsworthy, Devon

October 1967
That same month between Okehampton and Holsworthy, Devon, two uniformed officers observed a pulsating "flying cross-shaped" UFO moving at a low altitude. A fourteen-mile-long, high-speed pursuit followed during which the UFO made no noise and was seen to stop and hover. Later, a second UFO was seen.

1975

SALSFOR DOCKS

August 1975 at 0150 hours

In August at 0150 hours in Salsfor Docks, a patrolman walking his beat became aware of a large oval-shaped UFO approaching him. The object came to within thirty meters of his location and hovered over a nearby amenity block. No sound was heard coming from the UFO. After a short time, the UFO made a right turn and moved to a position over another building, where it remained for several minutes before shooting into the sky at an angle and at a tremendous speed.

OTHER REPORTS (FOUND ON THE INTERNET)

DEVON, ENGLAND

The following report is from the Internet, which was originally published in *The Times*, from Wales and Westcountry by Julian Mounter:

> On October 24th, in 1967, two constables witnessed an object that looked like a flying cross in Devon, England. They say they were watched by the object for about fifty minutes. At one point the constables tried to chase the object at speeds up to ninety miles per hour.
>
> *(The object) appeared to the left of us, then went in an arc and dipped down, and we thought it had landed. It seemed to be watching us and wouldn't let us catch up. It was at various altitudes all the time, but mostly just above the trees. It had terrific acceleration. It seemed to know we were chasing it.*
>
> They said it was not an airplane or a helicopter, but it was as large as a conventional aircraft. They tried to get closer to the object, but could not get any nearer than about 400 yards. Before it finally disappeared from sight, it was joined by a second object shaped like a cross, which was extremely bright and also silent.[46]

BRAZIL

The following article appeared on the Internet and was originally published in the daily newspaper *Diario La Regiao*, in Brazil on August 3, 1977:

ROAD POLICEMEN ALSO
SAW THE "FLYING SAUCER"

The strange luminous object – of large proportions and looking like a flying saucer – was also seen in late afternoon by the state road policemen Edson Pereira, currently on duty in Monte Aprasivel. What he told corresponds to the story told by Adimar Pablo Senaguedes and Antonio Tridico (Jaboran), of Rio Preto Telision.

According to Pereira, he returned to Rio Preto at 6 p.m., and sighted a strange object flying over the region emitting a strong light. It appeared to be silver-plated, as is described in relation to other objects that are sometimes called "flying saucers." The device performed very fast maneuvers and disappeared in the direction of Mirassol. Pereira stated:

It could not have been an airplane or a helicopter. The light was very strong, even strange. I never saw anything like this before.

He went to Mirassol airport and inquired if some device had gone down. The answer: "No airplane landed here."

Yesterday, when reading the story of the employee of Black River TV, Pereira declared: "the details coincide."

As it is remembered, Adimar and Jaboran saw the strange luminous object when they returned from Barreros and when they were 40 kilometers of distance to Sao Jose do Rio Preto when they saw a strange light evolving [revolving?] in our skies, at an incredible speed.[47]

FRANCE

The following article, also from the Internet, has been published in regional daily newspaper *L'Alsace, haut-Rhin*, Alsace, France, on September 20, 1998 in the general information section:

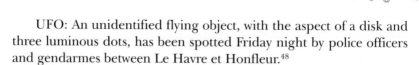

UFO: An unidentified flying object, with the aspect of a disk and three luminous dots, has been spotted Friday night by police officers and gendarmes between Le Havre et Honfleur.[48]

ARGENTINA

The following information was found at the web site listed below, and was taken from the local newspaper in Argentina.

TWO POLICEMEN SEE AND SHOOT
VIDEO OF UFO AND FOUR
SMALL HUMANOID FIGURES

On Sunday, November 18, 2007, two policemen out on patrol spotted an unusual light headed toward them as they were parked in their patrol truck. Using his cell phone camera, one of the officers took the video of four humanoids that were in front of him.

One of the officers said, "At that time I was loading a telephone calling card into my cell phone, and for that reason I remained in the vehicle. While I stared at the phone in my hand, I saw a small light, like that of a pickup truck approaching, but when I saw that it was closing in quickly, the light became larger as though from a large pickup truck. I wasn't disturbed by the scene, but at a distance of ten meters I saw a shape moving, and my first thought was that it was a dog. Then I saw that it was a silhouette, like that of a little man, standing approximately eighty centimeters tall, with a large head, large prominent gray eyes, and a greenish cast. I then tried to dial my fellow officer's cell phone, but when I pressed the 1 and the 5, my hand remained sort of static. I could see that three more creatures came out of that vehicle or craft, two similar to the first and a fourth with a slightly more robust appearance.[49]

FRANCE

The following article also appeared in the Internet, and was originally published in the daily newspaper *France Soir, France*, on September 13, 1995.

A UFO HOVERS ABOVE
A POLICEMAN'S CAR

Did the extraterrestrials appear yesterday morning in the sky of Perigueux? That is the claim of city police officer Christian Eytier, 34, who is in charge of an important police station of the suburbs of this city.

At about 6:30, while driving my car, in company of my daughter and a neighbor's kid, coming from my home, I saw a curious luminous object above us which followed us during five to six kilometers. A driver of a lorry, my daughter, and my neighbor saw it too.

I can insist that I was sober, for I do not put alcohol in my coffee. But, this time, I preferred to report it with the gendarmerie, qualified in this kind of matter. I remember a rectangle surrounded by luminous balls and equipped with a sort of projector which emitted rays.

The "spaceship" flew above his car, sometimes at a hundred meters height, at other times much lower, circling and zigzagging above the trees that border the road.[50]

POLICE CHASES

One of the many routine aspects of police work is the pulling over of a vehicle while on patrol. There are many reasons an officer might do this, and they use their judgment. However, if a driver ignores an officer's order to pull over and stop, the officer must make a snap decision. Is the pursuit worth the risks, both to the driver being chased and to the officer himself?

If the risk is not worthy of the chase, the officer can just get the license number and look for the driver at the address on record for the owner of the vehicle. However, if the officer decides that the driver should be apprehended right away, he can call for assistance and continue the chase.

The decision to call off a chase might be made for many reasons. On at least one occasion, it was made because the vehicle being pursued was flying and unidentifiable.

SOUTH AFRICA

The following is based on an article printed off the Internet. This one did not indicate a previous printing from a newspaper article. It was written by Jeff Love:

POLICE CHASE A UFO ABOVE
THE CAPITAL OF SOUTH AFRICA

On August 28, 1996, police chased a UFO in the vicinity of Pretoria, South Africa. At 4 a.m., Sgt. Johan Becker of the Adrian Volk Police Station in the suburb of Centurion saw a light flying in the sky which looked like a disc-shaped object with glowing red triangular lights. The police received many calls about the UFO, and officers were sent out over the area. The police watched the UFO for ninety minutes and one officer recorded the object on videotape.

At 5:30 a.m., a police helicopter was sent out to find the object being observed. The helicopter chased the object for a short time as it moved northwards toward a farming country at high speed. The helicopter climbed to a height of 3,000 meters, and eventually gave up the pursuit.

The evening television news interviewed the helicopter pilot, who stated that he and the others on board the helicopter believed that the object was not an aircraft but a genuine UFO.[51]

WARREN COUNTY, OHIO POLICE TAPES

The following is a transcript received by John Colaw, director of The UFO Disclosure, a UFO Internet bulletin board. Special thanks go to the late Kenny Young from Kentucky, who did a tremendous job investigating this case as well as some of the others in this book.

TRANSCRIPT OF TAPES

Note: The police tapes of the April 24th incident were acquired on May 15, 2001, from Carol Sigler, Warren County Director of Emergency Services, after written request to her office. The tapes were assembled from various "tracks" and edited for brevity and privacy considerations, and also arranged in presumed chronological order.

SECTION 1: INITIAL CALL

WCCC = Warren County Communications Center

WCCC Dispatcher #1:
Warren County Police and fire, this is Jesse?

Lebanon Dispatcher:
Hey this is Lebanon, P.D.

WCCC Dispatcher #1:
Hey.

Lebanon Dispatcher
Did you get any reports of UFOs in the area today?

WCCC Dispatcher #1:
Not yet, how about you?

Lebanon Dispatcher:
Huh? Yeah!

WCCC Dispatcher #1:
Oh really?

0 0 0

Lebanon Dispatcher:
Actually from a lady on Wilkerson Lane in Waynesville, to the far, far south of her, she sees a bright colored disk.

WCCC Dispatcher #1:
Oooh!

Lebanon Dispatcher:
And I'm not sure where Wilkerson Road is but I'm going to let my guys know about it to see if they see anything but I wondered if you had any reports.

WCCC Dispatcher #1:
Wilkerson Road, did she give her address anywhere?

Lebanon Dispatcher:
4636; she said it's been there for awhile and it's not doing anything.

WCCC Dispatcher #1:
She said she's seen a disk in the area?

Lebanon Dispatcher:
It's a bright... She thought it was a plane at first but she says it's a bright colored disk.

WCCC Dispatcher #1:
Okay.

Lebanon Dispatcher:
Allrighty.

WCCC Dispatcher #1:
I'll send the officers out that way to look.

SECTION 2:
DISPATCH

WCCC Dispatcher #2:
Two-William-30 a UFO!

Unit #2W30:
Go ahead.

WCCC Dispatcher #2:
4-6-3-6 Wilkerson Road, 4636 Wilkerson Road, the complaint apparently called the Lebanon P.D., advising they see a bright colored disk in the sky.

Unit #2W30
(*Laughing*): ... Clear!

WCCC Dispatcher #2:
Do your clear at 22:17.

Unit #2W30:
This is Unit number Two-William-30, what was the address on that UFO?

WCCC Dispatcher #2:
4-6-3-6- Wilkerson Road, 4636 Wilkerson Road; this is back a long lane straight off of Wilkerson Road between South Main Street and the dead end.

Unit #2W30:
Clear.

SECTION 3:
CITIZEN COMPLAINT

WCCC Dispatcher #3:
Warren County Police and Fire, Tonya?

Complaint:
Oh, this is Warren County?

WCCC Dispatcher #3:
Yes Ma'am.

Complaint:
I had just called Lebanon; we were wondering if anyone had reported anything in the sky, there is a light over to the south here and it's not moving and we were wondering if anybody had reported any strange thing.

WCCC Dispatcher #3:
You're at 4636 Wilkerson?

Complaint:
Yeah, you got it.

WCCC Dispatcher #3:
Okay, Lebanon had just called us with the information and we've got an officer on the way out to check it out. It's in the sky to the south of you?

Complaint:
Yeah, it's still there. Is he coming out here?

WCCC Dispatcher #3:
He's coming out to the area to see if he can see what you're seeing.

Complaint:
Oh, well okay.

WCCC Dispatcher #3:
Allrighty.

Complaint:
Sure, thank you. Bye bye.

SECTION 4:
VERIFICATION BY OFFICERS

WCCC Dispatcher #2:
Two-William-30, Two-William-31, 3-7 at 22:23, Unit #2W30 break. We've "public service" the residence and they advise the object is stationary in the sky.

Unit #2W30:
Okay…

WCCC Dispatcher #2:
Just south of the residence, in the sky.

Unit #2W30:
Hey Brad, check back in there to see if that's 4636.

0 0 0

Local:
William-30, Robert-50 Local. William-30, Robert-50 Local.

Unit #2W30:
Go ahead Local.

Local:
Okay, I gotta ask.

Unit #2W30:
Okay, uh… Yeah. Are you tied up?

Local:
WHAT IS IT!?

Unit #2W30:
I have NO IDEA, and you wouldn't believe it if you came out and saw it! There's two of them, just sitting stationary and blinking, I mean about five different colors, right here on Wilkerson, just off of South Main Street!

Female Officer:
This is 480-16…

Unit #2W30:
I'm not kidding! … Go ahead.

Female Officer:
Okay, we're on the backside of that, here in the lot because I can't stand it no more. Where is it at, is it in the air?

Unit #2W30:
In the air! Okay? He's got… The owner of the house has some binoculars and we're looking at these things and uh, it's just… I don't know what they are! They're high up, they look like… Uh, they're up there… But with our binoculars though, the one he's got here, you can see them pretty clearly. There's probably five different colors; there's two of them and they've stayed in the exact same spot the whole time. They're not stars, I can tell you that.

Female Officer:
This is 480-16, can we come back there with you? We are enroute and have spotted what you're talking about.

Unit #2W30:
I have no idea what it is.

Local:
Okay, I'm looking that way from the office and I can't see anything from up here.

Unit #2W30:
Okay, now there's a plane flying over right where it would be, I don't know if you could see that or not.

Local:
Does the plane have flashing red lights?

Unit #2W30:
Now right behind that to the left of it a little bit, that's it.

Local:
Would it be below the plane?

Unit #2W30:

Well the plane is directly overhead of us now, so I can't really tell.

Local:

Okay, I can tell the plane you are talking about but from up here I can't see anything else but a star.

Unit #2W30:

You wouldn't believe it.

Local:

Can you see that with your eyes or do you have to use binoculars to see it?

Unit #2W30:

I can see the flashing and everything with my eyes, you get the binoculars and you can really see it.

Local:

I think I know what you're talking about; I'm going to see if I can see it with my pair of binoculars.

Unit #2W30:

It looks like an orange, kind of a blue, a purple and a red almost with a green.

Female Officer:

Are you straight back toward the house?

Unit #2W30:

Come all the way back here, way back on the right, you'll see us standing here on the wall.

Female Officer:

All the way back up by the picnic?

Unit #2W30:

I see your lights now.

Female Officer:

Okay.

Local:

You're got some pretty lights, anyway.

Unit #2W30:

You see it now?

Local:

Affirmative, I've got a small pair of binoculars; I can definitely see the different colored lights anyway.

Unit #2W30:

Yeah, that's really... Uhhh... The resident's told me they've never seen it before so it's not like it's been there before.

Local:

Okay, there's two of them, right?

Unit #2W30:

The other one is just a little higher to the right of the one that's low, or right by the treeline.

Local:
> I'm not gonna call it.

Unit #2W30:
> I'm not either; I'm not going to even go there. But I… I don't know what it is.

Local:
> I can get blue, green red, and white lights is what I'm seeing.

Unit #2W30:
> That's what I am seeing.

Local:
> But we're not really seeing anything.

SECTION 5:
WCCC INQUIRY W/WPAFB

(WPAFB = Wright Patterson Air Force Base)

WPAFB:
> Operator?

WCCC Dispatcher #3:
> Hi, this is Tonya; I'm a Warren County Police and Fire dispatch?

WPAFB:
> Yeah.

WCCC Dispatcher #3:
> We've got Waynesville officers out in the area of Wilkerson Road and they see an object in the sky… a disk shape with multi-colored lights that is stationary in the air. Do you have somebody doing maneuvers down here?

WPAFB:
> And where are you?

WCCC Dispatcher #3:
> Warren County. He's in Waynesville and I'm in Lebanon.

WPAFB:
> No, we don't have anybody out there as far as I know.

WCCC Dispatcher #3:
> Okay.

WPAFB:
> Allright.

WCCC Dispatcher #3:
> Okay, thank you. Bye bye.

SECTION 6:
O.S.P. DISPATCH

WCCC Dispatcher #2:
> We called Wright Pat, they don't have anybody in the area doing maneuvers or anything. Okay at 22:35.

Unit #2A51:
Two-Adam-51?

WCCC Dispatcher #2:
Two-Adam-51.

Unit #2A51:
I'm out here with him.

WCCC Dispatcher #2:
3-7, 22:35. Two-William-30?

Unit #2W30:
Two-William-30, go ahead.

WCCC Dispatcher #2:
For your information, we also notified the O.S.P. in reference to the incident.
WCCC Dispatcher #3:
I've got "The State."

O.S.P. Dispatcher:
State Patrol, this is Taylor.

WCCC Dispatcher #3:
Hi, it's Tonya, over at "the County." I've got a UFO for you.

O.S.P. Dispatcher:
(*Laughing*)

WCCC Dispatcher #3:
I'm serious.

O.S.P. Dispatcher:
I know you are; I've been hearing stuff on the scanner.

WCCC Dispatcher #3:
They say if it's in the air, baby, it's yours!

O.S.P. Dispatcher:
So where's it at? (*Laughs*)

WCCC Dispatcher #3:
4636 Wilkerson Avenue.

O.S.P. Dispatcher:
Has it landed?

WCCC Dispatcher #3:
No, it hasn't landed. The only "little green man" is the Waynesville officer that's out there.

O.S.P. Dispatcher:
Has he seen it?

WCCC Dispatcher #3:
Yeah, they're adamant... It's in the air and it's got multicolored lights and stuff on it. There's two of them. We've called Wright Pat; they're not doing maneuvers. We don't know what it is.

O.S.P. Dispatcher:
All right, I'll send them.

WCCC Dispatcher #3:
But it's yours!

0 0 0

O.S.P. Dispatcher:
Like what are we going to do if it is a UFO?

WCCC Dispatcher #3:
Hey, I can call the National UFO Reporting Center, or better yet, give you the number.

O.S.P. Dispatcher:
"MOO-FOO!" It's "Moo-Foo" or something like that, isn't it? "Moo-Foo!" Ha! All right, I'll call them in just a second.

WCCC Dispatcher #3:
All right, bye.

O.S.P. Dispatcher:
Bye.

SECTION 7:

INQUIRY W/ WILMINGTON
AIRPORT/AIRBORNE EXPRESS

WCCC Dispatcher #2:
Two-William-30?

Unit #2W30:
Two-William-30.

WCCC Dispatcher #2:
Do you have an update on your UFO? Post 83 is responding and they're requesting an update.

Unit #2W30:
Okay, ahh... They're still there.

WCCC Dispatcher #2:
That's clear. Are you seeing two objects?

Unit #2W30:
Affirmative.

WCCC Dispatcher #2:
Okay, that's clear.

[WCCC contacts AIRBORNE EXPRESS located in Wilmington, Ohio (Clinton County) and listens as the call is routed through a push-button voice menu selection before being transferred to an attendant]

Airborne Operator:
Airborne Operator?

WCCC Dispatcher #3:
Hi, this is the Warren County Dispatch Center; I need to speak with your Air Traffic Controllers, please.

Airborne Operator:
One moment please.

Lisa:
Flight Control, this is Lisa.

WCCC Dispatcher #3:
Hi, this is Tonya; I'm a Warren County Police and Fire Dispatcher. I need to know if you've got any planes in the area of Waynesville that are stationary.

Lisa:
Um, probably not, but if you hold on I'll let you talk to the "Supe."

WCCC Dispatcher #3:
Thanks.

Bill:
Flight Control, Bill.

WCCC Dispatcher #3:
Hi, I'm a Warren County Police and Fire Dispatcher and we've got two unidentifiable objects in the air, in the area of Waynesville. Do you have two planes or any planes that are stationary?

Bill:
Let's see here, just a second. (*Steps away from the phone to check either radar or other records*)

WCCC Dispatcher #3:
Wright Pat is denying everything; they're saying they don't have anything up there. Like they're going to tell me, yeah right.
This is a Stealth Bomber and we're going to blow Corwin to blazes!"

Bill:
Ah, no. Right now we don't have any aircraft over that way. We have them east of Wilmington so we don't have anything over that way.

WCCC Dispatcher #4:
Dispatch, Lori?

O.S.P. Dispatcher:
Did you guys call anybody about the UFO?

WCCC Dispatcher #4:
Who's this?

O.S.P. Dispatcher:
State Patrol.

WCCC Dispatcher #4:
Yes, we did.

O.S.P. Dispatcher:
Who'd you call?

WCCC Dispatcher #4:
Airborne and Wright-Pat.

O.S.P. Dispatcher:
I mean like... UFO people?

WCCC Dispatcher #4:
No.

O.S.P. Dispatcher:
I'm embarrassed to call them.

WCCC Dispatcher #4:
Robert Fisse [spelling?], the Park Ranger, just called and said he can see them just fine. He said they appeared to be a great distance off but he could see them. He named the colors he could see.

O.S.P. Dispatcher:
Blue and green.

WCCC Dispatcher #4:
And red and white.

O.S.P. Dispatcher:
I guess I better call somebody then. Oh Lordy.

WCCC Dispatcher #4:
All right. Bye.

SECTION 8:

FURTHER OBSERVATION

Unit #2W30:
They just contacted O.S.P. I guess and Wright Pat doesn't have anything in the area; I don't know, this is weird.

Unknown Officer:
You got any tape on it?

Unit #2W30:
I don't even want to say. It's definitely round. Did you copy that?

Unknown Officer:
Yeah, we got it.

Unit #2W30:
(*Laughing*) Hey, I'm just telling you!

Unknown Officer:
Yeah, they're definitely not moving.

Unit #2W30:
Well, the one is now. It's moving farther and farther away... Well there it goes. It just stopped again.

Unknown Officer:
I don't want to know.

Unit #2W30:
Okay.

Unknown Officer:
I was just up here at the office doing paperwork and I had to check on it.

Unit #2W30:
No problem. I have 16-Robert-50 on local, ah, Paul Rohrer [spelling?] just spotted one right above you. It's coming real close. (*Breaks into laughter*)

Unknown Officer:
Okay wonderful. Ah, all I got's a plane right up here that I can see.

Unit #2W30:
> It's a plane and then it's... I don't know. I don't know. I thought I'd let you know.

Unknown Officer:
> I can still see the other two, but I don't see any third one.

Unit #2W30:
> This is actually coming from where you're at.

Unknown Officer:
> All right, I don't see that one. Ah, I called the Com-Center on the phone and told them that if they went outside they could probably see it.

Unit #2W30:
> Okay, are they seriously sending O.S.P. out here?

Unknown Officer:
> I assume they are. O.S.P. has contacted Wright Pat apparently. (**Note**: Incorrect, WCCC contacted Wright Pat.)

Unit #2W30:
> Okay.

Unknown Officer:
> They checked with them; I don't know if they're actually going to have them come to your location or what.

SECTION 9:
CONTINUED DISCUSSION

WCCC Dispatcher #4:
> Dispatch, Lori.

O.S.P. Dispatcher:
> Hey, Lori, this is Lori.

WCCC Dispatcher #4:
> Yep.

O.S.P. Dispatcher:
> What's your latest update; are they still there?

WCCC Dispatcher #4:
> Yeah, they're still there and they still have a visual on it.

O.S.P. Dispatcher:
> Damn! You know, I've called just about every number I could find on UFOs but these numbers are so damned old!

WCCC Dispatcher #4:
> Have you got a unit enroute up there?

O.S.P. Dispatcher:
> Yeah, I have two.

WCCC Dispatcher #3:
> Tell them to capture it; tell them to lasso it and pull it down.

O.S.P. Dispatcher:
>Well, what they're going to do is film it so we can see it later.

WCCC Dispatcher #3:
>Okay.

O.S.P. Dispatcher:
>Okay, bye.

Lisa:
>This is Lisa.

Unit #2W30:
>Lisa...

Lisa:
>Yes...

Unit #2W30:
>This is Two-William-30...

Lisa:
>Yes...

Unit #2W30:
>What is going on?

Lisa:
>Well I don't know, you're out there looking at it, what is it?

Unit #2W30:
>Ahh... I couldn't tell you.

Lisa:
>Is there really something there though?

Unit #2W30:
>I can tell you it's not a plane and it's not a star.

LISA:
>It's not a plane and it's not a star...?

Unit #2W30:
>No, it's round and it's got... Wait a second, O.S.P. is on the scene.

Lisa:
>Anything in the air... I don't know if you know this or not, but anything in the air or falls from the air is State Patrol's jurisdiction. Evidently, you didn't know that because we could hear your side traffic but we had to tell that that's procedure. Anything in the air or falls from the air is State Patrol but that's... Where are you at, where you can see it? Is it like right over you or...?

Unit #2W30:
>No, it's in the distance toward Hamilton.

Lisa:
>Towards Hamilton?

Unit #2W30:
>Yeah, O.S.P.'s here; I'll have to give you a call back.

Lisa:
Okay.

SECTION 10:

WCCC DISPATCHER OBSERVES UFO

NORTH OF HER LOCATION

O.S.P. Dispatcher #2:
Highway State Patrol Dispatcher Hussman [spelling?].

WCCC Dispatcher #5:
Hey Kim...

O.S.P. Dispatcher #2:
Yeah.

WCCC Dispatcher #5:
What are they saying about that UFO?

O.S.P. Dispatcher #2:
I don't know yet.

WCCC Dispatcher #5:
I can see it from here. It's got a light blue light, a yellow light, and a red light alternating, flashing on it and it looks like it's in a line. If I step out... not the door that we normally come in but that other basement door... walk to the top of the steps and look at [Route] 48, it's to the left, way up in the sky up like toward my house... toward Waynesville.

O.S.P. Dispatcher #2:
We're still trying to find phone numbers.

WCCC Dispatcher #5:
For what?

O.S.P. Dispatcher #2:
To get a hold of somebody.

WCCC Dispatcher #5:
We've got the UFO numbers.

O.S.P. Dispatcher #2:
Tell me what you've got, because everything we've got isn't any good.

[Radio traffic from other police officers heard in background, they assure the object is not a plane and not a star]

O.S.P. Dispatcher #2:
It's not a plane and it's not a star, they're saying, and it's not moving.

WCCC Dispatcher #5:
It didn't move when I was looking at it. (*Calls out for Tonya to find UFO number*) Here it is, National UFO Reporting Center, 206-722-3000. That's in Seattle.

O.S.P. Dispatcher #2:
That's who we're on the phone with and they said if it's the only one, it could be a Sirius star.

0 0 0

WCCC Dispatcher #5:
It's got a light blue, a yellow and a red flashing light on it.

O.S.P. Dispatcher #2:
(*Repeats to attendant in room to convey to NUFORC – National UFO Reporting Center*) She said it's got a light blue, a yellow, and a red flashing light on it, and they're in a straight line.

WCCC Dispatcher #5:
Well if it's like in a circle, I'm only seeing... It's not the same light alternating flash, it's in different locations, like the light blue is in the middle, the red flashes on the right and the yellow flashes on the left of the light blue light, and the light blue light stays constant.

O.S.P. Dispatcher #2:
The light blue light is in the middle.

WCCC Dispatcher #5:
Correct. And from where I'm looking at it, the red is on the right and the yellow is on the left, and they flash. The light blue light flashes but it's almost like it's flickering. The other one's you just see alternately. Trying looking at it, it's different! I mean they're not flashing, it's not the same light changing colors, it's like three different locations on a straight line. Right on the same thing, you can tell it's the same thing. And it doesn't look like it's up as far as a star would be, but it's higher than a plane would be, and it's stationary.

O.S.P. Dispatcher #2:
(*Laughter*)

WCCC Dispatcher #5:
What?

O.S.P. Dispatcher #2:
We just talked to them at that National UFO Hotline?

WCCC Dispatcher #5:
Yeah?

O.S.P. Dispatcher #2:
They just told her that last January several departments in Illinois chased after a triangular-shaped UFO for several miles...

WCCC Dispatcher #5:
...and then...?

O.S.P. Dispatcher #2:
Nothing.

WCCC Dispatcher #5:
It disappeared?

O.S.P. Dispatcher #2:
There's nothing they could do!

WCCC Dispatcher #5:
Well, what good are they? So we can't get anybody to see if they can get this on radar or anything?

O.S.P. Dispatcher #2:
Our guys are filming it.

WCCC Dispatcher #5:
Oh, are they?

O.S.P. Dispatcher #2:
They're trying to.

WCCC Dispatcher #5:
Okay... Well, I just wondered what your status was with it.

O.S.P. Dispatcher #2:
So far, that's it.

WCCC Dispatcher #5:
So the UFO Center is thinking it's possibly a Sirius star?

O.S.P. Dispatcher #2:
Yes.

WCCC Dispatcher #5:
With those color lights?

O.S.P. Dispatcher #2:
Yes.

WCCC Dispatcher #5:
I don't think so, but okay.

O.S.P. Dispatcher #2:
They said if it's one, it's a Sirius star, but if there's two, it's not a Sirius star.

WCCC Dispatcher #5:
Okay, bye.

SECTION 11:
FINAL CONVERSATION

Local:
William-30, Robert-50. There's also one to the north.

Unit #2W30:
Okay, you see one now?

Local:
Yeah, I see from our direction from you and to the north a little bit.

Unit #2W30:
Yeah, that's the one I think we're looking at and I have no clue what it is.

Local:
Well, at first I'd say it was just stars through the atmosphere, but the ones that are lower than that doesn't look like those.

Unit #2W30:
No, from where we're at with the binoculars that we got, this isn't a star, I can tell you that much. And it's not a plane, I can definitely rule those out, too.

Local:
Yeah, I've got some real small glasses up here and can see all the colors but can't make out any form.

Unit #2W30:
I'm calling Com-Center now and see what's going on.

Local:
Okay, so what have you got? William-30, Robert-50, William-30, Robert-50. William-30, Robert-50. What's he ending up with?

Unknown Officer:
I think it's wishful thinking; I don't think it's much. It's some sparkling lights, I think it's a plane or something, but I don't know

Local
(*Laughing*) Okay, you're clear.

Unit #2W30:
16 to Robert-50, he just needed to get his eyes re-examined because – like I said – this isn't a plane and it's not a star.

Local:
Yeah, I sat up here watching it for awhile and if it's a plane, it's not moving.

Unknown Officer:
You guys have been watching too many *X-Files* movies.

Unit #2W30:
16 to Robert-50, do you still have a good visual on it?

Local:
I'm up by "4-3" now and I can't see anything from up here. When I left the park over there, I could still see two of them, anyway.

Unit #2W30:
Okay.

Local:
I'll leave them into your capable hands and trust you'll keep it safe tonight. I'm going "A.W."

Unit #2W30:
Okay, I'm going to leave this to the State, to O.S.P. to handle, so I'm "A.W." also.

Local:
You're clear.

Report/transcript prepared by Kenny Young
May 24, 2001

FOUR POLICE OFFICERS TRACK UFO

Two police officers in the Gladstone, Michigan police department were sent to investigate a UFO sighting called into the station during the early morning hours on the 12th of March 1980. They expected to find a simple, prosaic explanation for the UFO, as they have done many times in the past.

"We've had reports of UFOs and stuff like that before," one of the officers stated. "They usually turn out to be airplanes or planets or something."

When they arrived, they saw something they had never encountered before. The object had a bright white light, two red lights on each side and a green light near the back. They could not make out any shape because it was too dark.

While they were there, they were joined by two officers from the Delta County Sheriff's Department. They had also received a number of calls about the object, and had been sent out to investigate. As the four men watched, the object started moving and the officers followed as best they could for about a half hour until they lost it.

Not too far away, two police officers from the Escanaba Police Department saw and reported a similar object.[52]

PORTAGE COUNTY, OHIO POLICE CHASE

On April 17th of 1966, a UFO chase took place that involved nine police officers over five counties and three states, and was seen by hundreds of witnesses.

Two Portage County deputy sheriffs, Dale Spaur and Wilbur "Barney" Neff, were driving on Route 224 at 5 a.m., when they noticed a car parked off the road near a large field. The car attracted their attention because it had an unusual number of antennas on it, so they stopped and got out of their patrol car to investigate. As they were approaching the car, Spaur looked over his shoulder to make sure no one was sneaking up on them and saw a brightly lit craft rise up from the nearby field. He motioned to Neff to look and after they both observed the object for a few moments, they decided to get back into their car. They estimated that the object was about fifty to seventy feet in diameter and about fifteen to twenty feet in height.

They radioed back to the Sheriff's office and reported what they had seen and were ordered to stay with the craft and watch it until an officer with a camera could get there to take some pictures. The lighted craft began to move slowly, crossing the street and moving east. As the object

started to move, they radioed the dispatcher that it was leaving and asked for permission to follow it. They were given permission to do so.

While they pursued the object, another deputy was also watching the light in the sky. He reported that the lights were about one half mile away and that the object was about 100 feet in the air before he joined the other two in the chase. The object and the deputies were now going about 80 to 90 miles per hour, and the object rose to about 500 feet in altitude. As their speed approached 100 miles per hour, the officers turned on their lights and sirens in order to prevent any accidents with pedestrians or other vehicles. The noise of the sirens woke residents in the area, and they looking out their windows to see the object in the sky being followed by two police cars on the ground. Spaur reported that, at one point as they were driving under a bridge, they seemed to lose the object, but it was there on the other side, almost as if waiting for them.

Two more officers, Officer Wayne Huston of the East Palestine police and Officer Frank Paanzanella in Conway County, now joined the chase. The dispatcher in Conway County notified the Pittsburgh Airport, who notified the Air Force, who in turn scrambled two jets. However, the object was traveling too slowly for the jets to maintain altitude, so they circled around and returned to their base. A few days later, the Air Force denied ever scrambling the jets.

As they got into Pennsylvania near the Pittsburgh Airport, the officers stopped as the object stopped and appeared to hover. It then moved to a higher elevation, estimated at 1,300 feet, although the airport radar operator reported that nothing showed up on his radar screen. Two more fighter jets with missiles were launched by the Air Force, and then the object suddenly moved higher and out of sight.

The Air Force's Project Blue Book, which looked into this, concluded that all of the officers saw the planet Venus. The five officers responded that they were able to see the object close to the ground and at one point they saw it cross the sky right in front of both the moon and Venus.[53]

UFO Filmed By Cops
Just Bright Spot

At 9:15 p.m., on Monday night, the 14th of November, 1973, two police officers responded to a report of lights in the sky. "We went to investigate," said one of the officers. "...and as we approached ...we saw a bluish white object, real bright which appeared to be dropping at a 45-degree angle. It stopped and hovered for a brief period at a low altitude."

As they approached the object, it moved higher in elevation at a 45-degree angle to about 1,000 to 1,500 feet. It hovered there for a few moments and then started to move away. The two officers started to chase the object at speeds of about 70 miles per hour until they lost it.

While chasing the object one officer took a picture of the object, but when they had the film developed, all they could see was a bright blip on the film.[54]

ALBANY, NEW YORK

August 20, 1974

At approximately 8 p.m., an object with a red light was seen traveling north along the Northway near the Round Lake area. The object was picked up by radar at the Albany County Airport and was visually spotted by a State Trooper from his patrol car. At one point, the object was traveling at approximately 3,600 MPH, according to the Albany Airport control tower. The patrolman estimated that he saw it moving about 100 MPH. It had stood still in the air about 200 feet above the patrol car for a brief time, then left.

Two small military planes were sent by the airport to get a better observation from the air. The pilots of the planes informed the air traffic control operators that they could see the police and a small trailer park but they could not see the UFO. The state police reported that they could look up and see the airplanes and the UFO. While the planes were visible on radar, the object was not. After the planes left, however, it once again appeared on the radar screen.

The air traffic control tower told state police that the object traveled about seventeen miles in sixteen seconds. There were six air traffic control operators, at least two military pilots, and at least two state troopers involved.[55]

Source: *Albany Times Union Newspaper* and a radio interview on WGY between John Wallace Spencer and one of the Air traffic controllers

UTAH

In the Utah Basin in the Eastern Part of Utah, Deputy Sheriff Bernard Hadden saw a brilliant light in the sky during the fall of 1996. He watched the light with binoculars from about a mile away, at an angle of 45 degrees. He could not discern any distinct shape, although he got the impression that it was of considerable size. It first seemed to be coming toward him, then changed direction, disappeared, came back into sight and finally left, moving from east to west.

0 0 0

Just south of Ft. Duchesne, Utah on October 24, 1966, Ute tribal police officers watched two lights about 15 degrees above the horizon in the Southeast. They reported that the lights were as brilliant as a blue-white welding torchlight, with colors changing to a yellowish hue and then fading. One object moved fast, then pulsated red and hovered. They watched the lights for over an hour with binoculars.

At ten o'clock p.m., on November 20, 1967, in Roosevelt, Utah, a police officer observed a round object with pulsating, rotating lights of red, green, and amber. It was moving slowly at first, and then increased its speed. He observed it through binoculars and could see that it was not an airplane, though he could not determine what it was. The object was only about 100 yards away, made no sounds and was making complex maneuvers.

On January 12, 1965, at Custer, Washington, a round illuminated craft landed on a farm near the Blaine Air Force Base. Apparently, it was the same thirty-foot flying disk which was tracked by Air Force radar as it swooped down to buzz the car of a federal law enforcement officer. Snow melted and the ground was scorched in a circular area where the UFO had landed. One witness said that the Air Force instructed him not to discuss the case.

Source: *The Utah UFO Display* by Frank Salisbury
The Devon – Adair Co. Publishers

EXETER, NEW HAMPSHIRE

In his book, *Incident at Exeter,* author and newspaper reporter, John G. Fuller describes an event that took place on September 3, 1965. John G. Fuller, you will note elsewhere on in this book, is also the author of *The Interrupted Journey,* a book about Betty and Barney Hill who had a very interesting sighting. Although they weren't the first to experience, they were probably the first to have documented an abduction in association with seeing a UFO.

In the early hours of the morning, 19-year-old Norman Muscarello was walking home when a "thing," as he called it, came out from a field nearby. It was at least as big as a house, about eighty or ninety feet in diameter and had pulsating red lights around the rim. Panicking, he ran out to the road and waved a traveling car to stop and take him into town. There he tried to tell the desk officer what he saw. A few minutes later, Officer Eugene Bertand returned to the station and accompanied

Muscarello back out to the area where the object was seen. Upon arrival, Bertrand radioed back that nothing was visible. Both men got out of the patrol car and walked out into the nearby field. Bertrand began to sweep the field with his flashlight trying to see anything, convinced that Muscarello must have seen a helicopter. A few minutes later, Muscarello yelled that he could see the object. Out across the field, a large round object rose without a sound from behind some trees and moved toward them. The entire area was bathed in a red light. Bertrand reached for his .38, then thought better of it and shoved it back into its holster. Muscarello froze in fear but Bertrand grabbed him and yanked him toward the police cruiser.

Back at the Exeter police station, Officer Toland, the on duty desk officer, was blasted out of his seat when Bertrand radioed back "My God. I can see the damn thing myself!" From inside the car they watched as the object hovered 100 feet above them and about 100 yards away. The pulsating red lights seemed to dim from right to left, then back and forth, and then from right to left again in a 5-4-3-2-1 and then 1-2-3-4-5 pattern. The object rocked back and forth on its axis, still absolutely silent.

Neither man could make out much of a definite shape because the lights were so bright. Bertrand said that it was like trying to describe a car with the headlights coming at you. It continued to hover for a few minutes then began to slowly move away, eastward. Its movement was erratic, defying all conventional aerodynamic patterns. "It darted," said Bertrand. It could turn on a dime and then it would slow down.

At that moment, Officer David Hunt pulled up to the area in his patrol car. "I could see that fluttering movement." Hunt said, "It was going from left to right, between the tops of two big trees. I could see those pulsating lights." After the object left the area and was out of sight, a B-47 came by and they could tell the difference. There was no comparison.

At the time that the object moved away, the night phone operator called the police station and spoke to Officer Toland. She was very excited. Some man had just called her and was so hysterical he could hardly talk straight. He told her that a flying saucer came right at him, but before he could finish telling her, he was cut off. She was able to trace the call to an outside phone booth in the Town of Hampton. She immediately phoned the Hampton Town Police, who called the Pease Air Force Base. The blotter at the Hampton Police department read:

Sept. 3. 1965: 3 a.m. Exeter Police Dept. reports unidentified flying object in that area. Units 2, 4 and Pease Air Force alerted. At 3:17 a.m., received a call from the Exeter operator and Officer Toland. Advised

that a male subject called and asked for police department, further stating that call was in re: a large unidentified flying object, but call was cut off. Call received from a Hampton pay phone, location unknown.

The next morning at eight o'clock police Lt. Cottrell read Bertrand's report and called the Pease Air Force Base to reconfirm the incident. The report said:

At 2:27 a.m., Officer Toland on duty at the desk called me into the station. Norman J Muscarello, 205 ½ Front Street was in the station and he was upset. He had told Officer Toland that on the way home from Amesbury, MA, in Kensington, NH, while walking along Rt. 150 an unidentified flying object came out of the sky with red lights on it.

He got down on the road so that it would not get him. Officer Toland sent me to this place where Muscarello had seen this thing.

The place was a field near Tel. Pole #668 on Route 150. I did not see anything.

I got out of the cruiser and went into the field and all of a sudden this thing came at me at about 100 feet off the ground with red lights going back and forth. Officer Hunt got there and also saw this thing. It had no motor and came through the air like a leaf falling from a tree. By the time Hunt got to this field, the UFO had gone over the trees, but he saw it.

(Signed) Ptl. E. Bertrand

After confirming the report with Lt. Cottrell, John Fuller wrote:

I talked with Lieutenant Cottrell, who told me that both Bertrand and Hunt were level-headed and calm, and not at all inclined to exaggerate. What's more, the station had been getting too many reports from too many reliable people to question the fact that something was being seen, and being seen regularly. "They're still coming in from all over," the lieutenant said. "And either you believe these people or call them nuts." Well, I know a lot of them and they definitely are not nuts. They're good, quiet respectable people who wouldn't be inclined to go around making up yarns like this. Now take Bertrand, for instance. He's one of the toughest boys on the force. We send him out on all the rough jobs. Not afraid of anything. But, boy he was scared this time. I will say this – if only one of these boys saw this thing, I might have taken the live ammunition out of his gun. Or if I had reason to doubt him and Hunt, I'd put 'em in the back room and give them some blocks to play with. And I'll tell you this much – if I had seen this thing the way they describe it, and I was alone, nobody else would've ever heard about it.[56]

In the same book, Fuller supplies a few more police sightings:

OKLAHOMA

On July 31, 1965, a police officer named Louis Sikes from Wynnewood, Oklahoma, reported a forty-five minute UFO sighting and both Tinker and Carswell Air Force bases came up with a fix on their radar. The night of August 1 was jammed with reports throughout the night. Three different Shawnee, Oklahoma, police cars reported diamond-shaped formations of UFOs for thirty to forty minutes, shortly after 9 p.m. They were said to be moving in a northerly direction and changing colors from red to white to blue-green, and at times moved from side to side. In Chickasha, first news of the sighting came from radio station KWCO, with James Cline, police dispatcher, confirming that he had a report from Patrolman C.V. Barnhill verifying them. In Oklahoma City, police dispatcher Lt. Homer Briscoe said police headquarters received over thirty-five calls between 8 p.m. and 10 p.m., with most of the estimated indicating that the objects were at an altitude of 15,000 to 20,000 feet.

"People are upset," Briscoe said. "They want to know what they are, and we can't tell them."

Meanwhile, the Oklahoma Highway Patrol headquarters was trying to keep its teletype clear, and sorting out the reports from all over the state:

It was reported that witnesses had called in about 50 visual sightings of the objects. Many of the sightings were by local police officers and Highway Patrol officers. They reported seeing various types of objects from the Purcell area through the Norman area to the Chandler area and back to Meaker and Shawnee areas.

Three of the officers from the Town of Shawnee reported seeing four of the objects. Another object was seen just south of Tecumseh and seems to be heading in the direction to fly directly through Shawnee.

The objects were reported in colors, starting at a reddish color and varying to a white and blue luster.

Witnesses, including many of the officers, reported that the objects seemed to be flying at about four objects to a formation and in a diamond-shaped pattern. Officer Cushing had reported seeing four of the objects.

Two units from the Highway Patrol reported seeing some of the objects, as well. Tinker Air Force Base reported that they had had from one to four of the objects on radar at a time. The base also reported that the objects were showing up on the radar at an elevation of about 22,000 feet which would confirm the sightings on the ground at a very high elevation.

TEXAS

On September 3, 1965 (the same day as the sighting in Exeter, New Hampshire) Chief Deputy Sheriff Billy McCoy and Deputy Sheriff Robert Goode were on patrol about forty miles south of Houston, Texas, when they noticed a bright purple light about five miles away. A few moments later they noticed a smaller bluer light near it. The lights then suddenly moved toward their cruiser. In their report to the Air Force, the two officers said:

> The object came up to the pasture next to the highway and about 150 feet off the highway and about 100 feet high. The bulk of the object was plainly visible and appeared to be triangular-shaped, with a bright purple light on the left side and on the smaller, less bright blue light on the right end. The bulk of the object appeared to be dark gray in color with no other distinguishing features. It appeared to be enormous – about 200 feet wide and 40-50 feet thick in the middle, tapering off toward both ends. There was no noise or any trail.

The bright purple light illuminated the ground directly underneath it and the area in front of it, including the highway and the interior of the patrol car. The tall grass under the object did not appear to be disturbed.

There was a bright moon out and it cast a shadow of the object on the ground immediately below it in the grass. Deputy Sheriff Goode was in the driver's seat with his left arm in the open window. Although he was wearing a long-sleeved shirt and a coat, he later said that he felt the heat emanating from the object.

The two men, shocked by the approach of the craft, drove away at 110 miles per hour. After they had gotten away, they wondered if the object was still there so they drove back to the area where they saw it. It was still there, so they drove away again to avoid another possible close encounter.

Fuller, also mentions that UFOs were reported hovering and bobbing over the northern and western Minneapolis suburbs. Robert Riley of the State Highway Patrol and three patrolmen observed the phenomenon in seven different communities nearby. A total of fifty police and sheriff squad cars radioed in reports between 12:20 a.m. and 2:30 a.m. on August 3, 1965.

VERMONT

One last account from *Incident At Exeter* concerns a Chief Medical Examiner of the College of Medicine at the University of Vermont, and a Vermont state trooper. At about 5:15 p.m., on the 4th of January 1965, while traveling on Highway 12, both men saw an orange-red light above a distant treetop. They said the light shone with an intensity somewhat less than an automobile headlight. It came in sight and crossed the highway in front of them. At arm's length it was about the size of a football field. They thought it looked round but could not be sure because of its great speed. As soon as it passed by, a second object, followed by a third, passed by in the same direction. The objects all climbed slightly, moving west to east, and faded out of sight over a valley to the right of the witnesses. The whole sighting lasted about thirty seconds. There was no sound and the speed was faster than a jet aircraft.

The doctor filed a report to the press and to the Vermont State Aeronautics Board. In his statement he said:

> I hesitated to call. I know everything I say will be open to misinterpretation. But remember, two of us saw the same thing at the same time. I was not seeing things, and I am not too overly imaginative and neither is the trooper.

At the time of the sighting, both of these men were on their way home after testifying to a grand jury. Their testimony was credible in the courtroom and there were also other witnesses in the area who saw the same sight and had come forward.[57]

GEORGIA UFO SIGHTINGS

The following reports were submitted to us by Tom Sheets, a retired police chief, who was also the State Director for MUFON in Georgia:

UNKNOWN OBJECT FLIES OVER POLICE CAR

3Feb00, about 4:00 a.m.

An officer/supervisor with a N.W. Georgia County Police Department was parked roadside doing some paperwork while waiting to begin traffic duties. He noticed a flying object approaching his position at high speed from the southeast. What first drew his attention was a red glow outlining a round shape. While trying to exit his vehicle for a

0 0 0

better look, he observed the unknown object swiftly fly almost directly over his squad car, giving him a relatively close view in which he could see the full outline and shape, then the red glow at the rear. He noticed it appeared grayish in color with no apparent markings or windows that he could see under those conditions, and it was about the size of a small house. The craft seemed to be spinning clockwise, then quickly flew out of sight. The witness was sure it was silent, and not a small airplane or helicopter or meteor, and that it was definitely a physical object. The Mutual UFO Network (MUFON) of Georgia interviewed this witness, visited the event site, and received excellent sketches from the witness. (Sketches – side profile reminds one of a 230 grain .45cal ACP projectile, with a more pointed nose than the standard rounded-off nose shape of such a projectile. Front view is round. Rear view is round with circular red glow).

This event was investigated by MUFON of Georgia FI Mary Dee Janssen.

CORRECTIONS OFFICER OBSERVES HUGE TRIANGULAR CRAFT OVER-FLY PRISON

Joint National UFO Reporting Center (NUFORC)/MUFON of Georgia Investigation 23Feb00 at about 10:55 p.m.

A Corrections Officer at a prison in east Georgia was on night patrol in his corrections van, securing the perimeter road around the facility. He noticed lights in the sky to the northeast, which appeared to be getting bigger/closer. He drove around to that side, parked and got out to watch more closely. The lights appeared to have moved swiftly closer, and were hovering over some woods about 1,000 yards away. He then noticed the lights were moving toward him at a slow, almost walking, speed and seemed about 1,000 feet in altitude. When the craft came very close, he identified it as looking like a very large dark "arrowhead" with lights outlining the two forward edges and a larger center light underneath. It silently passed overhead and the witness estimated that it was larger than an L-1011 passenger jet. From first distant observation, to the fly-over and departure, about thirty minutes elapsed. The officer called it in on his radio, but the Corrections dispatcher inside the facility humorously chided him about it. The witness provided a very good sketch of what he observed to MUFON of Georgia. Please note: During this same general time period, there

was a similar spectacular event of a giant triangle overflying Georgia's I-75 a few miles below Hartsfield Airport near Palmetto Georgia ...again, with another high-quality reliable witness (whose immediate family members were public safety supervisors i.e., police and fire/rescue). Additionally, there were many similar triangle reports from all over the eastern United States during that period.

This event was investigated by the Tom Sheets.

LARGE STAR-LIKE UFO ABSORBING SMALLER LIGHTS

Chief Investigator for Georgia MUFON Observes Dramatic Aerial Phenomenon During Investigation, 13Sept97, at about 9:32 p.m.

This writer was en route to a south Georgia county, the last of three such trips, to conclude an investigation. Earlier (instigating this investigation), municipal police officers in the county had reported unknown objects in their skies while on night patrol and off-duty. One such event involved an unknown craft hovering over the local airfield and another observed via a rifle scope. Another event involved a high-ranking police official, and others, while off-duty and fishing at night. These witnesses all reported seeing a bright star-like object absorbing a series of smaller glowing objects.

Tom Sheets was returning to south Georgia in order to conduct an all-night surveillance from the local airfield in that vicinity. When approaching the general area of these events at the above specified time, I was headed SE on Georgia Hwy 23/341 in the vicinity of McRae, Georgia, a largely rural, agricultural area. The weather was clear, with a few patchy, puffy, fair-weather clouds, mild temperatures, with a slight breeze from the south, basically outstanding CAVU (Ceiling And Visibility Unlimited, meaning excellent viewing conditions). While driving, I noticed some aircraft lights off to the south (right front) which were low on the horizon, perhaps one or two miles distant. As indicated, a few patchy clouds were floating by, one to the front and another further off to the right. The aircraft was flying lower than these patchy clouds, and toward me from the south. While looking at the aircraft and the clouds, an event unfolded which perplexes me to this day.

A "ray-like" light suddenly lit up the cloud in front, being silently emitted out from BEHIND it toward the direction of the approaching aircraft. When I say "emitted," what I mean is that it was like a switch was thrown and the immediate result was the thick ray-like light being projected as if from some hidden massive mechanical

device. The duration was two or more seconds, then suddenly it was gone, as if "clicked" off. I think my words cannot do it justice. I have in the past compared it to looking at the type of colors one might (fancifully) imagine exists inside a nuclear reaction... the most intense, brilliant, solid bluish-purple (ray), trimmed with a brilliant yellow-orange on the edges, against a startling accompanying background bluish glow. The ray was as thick as, or thicker than the appearance of the full moon low on the horizon, and extended out toward the aircraft and nearby smaller cloud at an approximate width of both side-by-side. Combine this with the bizarre quality of the colors being so INTENSE and so SOLID as if to look like a piece of high quality animation. They were brilliant, but not in the way of a lightning strike or lightning discharge. This event IN NO WAY RESEMBLED A LIGHTNING DISCHARGE OR FLASH. The beginning and end of the event was precise... as if a switch was thrown.

This writer quickly pulled off the roadway looking for the aircraft (or a crashing aircraft!!), grabbing binoculars. Once outside, the aircraft lights were again observed, still on course toward my position. An effort was made with the binoculars to pick out a registration number or markings in the glow of its lights as it flew over (small aircraft like a Piper Cub). This was not successful.

It should be noted that absolutely NO summer lightning flashes had been observed before this event, and NO such flashes were observed the remainder of the night... until about 6 a.m. or dawn. Efforts were later made to identify and locate the aircraft via local airport managers, the FAA, and others... all leading to nothing. This event was subsequently discussed with a meteorologist who indicated that lightning might take several forms, but he was at a loss to explain what was described to have occurred under those particular conditions.

Whether this means anything in the above described event or not, wanted to include it since IT HAS meant something in numerous past major case investigations... to include life or death situations. This writer spent fourteen years of his twenty-five-year law enforcement career as a major crimes and homicide investigator and CID Commander. During that twenty-five years, I would often get a certain "feeling" that would forewarn me of soon-to-be situations that were life threatening, and several times it alerted me, thereby causing extra caution etc., saving possible injury of death. This also worked during the investigation of a "whodunit," which later proved to be a contract murder. The "feeling" led to the recovery of hidden evidence, resulting in three arrests and convictions in that matter. There are other incidents like this, but that is a good example. This "feeling" was actually at work much earlier in 1967 in South Vietnam with the First Marine Division, when it led

to certain movements and actions that saved our unit from being surrounded during an ambush, and again in 1973, in the Patrol Division when I avoided being shot and thereafter shooting the gunman, DOA.

Forward to 1997. The afternoon of the last trip down to south Georgia described above, I was actually planning to drive down to the LaGrange, Georgia area to interview a witness in a case in our infamous "Troup-Heard UFO Corridor" of far west Georgia. While walking out the front door, FI [field investigation] kit in hand, thinking of our THC [[what is THC?]], my mind was suddenly changed for no reason I could discern... just suddenly decided to drive down to deep south Georgia and finish off the police officer's case. While driving, that old "feeling" was back again... like a pebble in a shoe... It stayed with me until my observation of that aerial event described above... Then it was gone... like exhaling a breath that I had been holding. Synchronicity at work? Don't know. But that old "feeling" has never been wrong. It even came into play during the Wayne Williams investigation, and while not solving the cases(s), it was later proved to be 100 percent correct.

From the
Bob Pratt Files
By Bob Pratt and Cynthia Luce

A UFO research pioneer, Bob Pratt, had investigated the following cases. We would like to express our gratitude to Mrs. Pratt for allowing us to include these cases of her late husband.

Bob had spent forty-eight years as a newspaper and magazine reporter and editor. As a newspaper reporter, Bob started out as a UFO skeptic. But after interviewing over sixty UFO witnesses in one week, Bob began to believe that there was something to this after all. He was the author of the book *UFO DANGER ZONE: Terror and Death in Brazil – Where Next?* And he co-authored the popular book *Night Siege: The Hudson Valley UFO Sightings.*

FOUR COPS SEE UFO

While I was working on the first Crab Island incident, in which a man died and two were burned, police officers told me about some sightings.

"I have some friends, four police officers, who were traveling to São Mateus and they saw something unusual in the sky," said Jucilmo Salazar Pereira, a police investigator for the state of Maranhão. São Mateus is a small city about two hundred kilometers south of São Luis.

"At first they thought it was the moon but the thing just stopped behind a *babaçu* tree and lit up the area. They radioed São Mateus and asked that someone be sent to see what they were seeing. The others came and saw it and after a while the thing disappeared."

Another detective, Orlando Arouce, said: "I have a neighbor, an old lady named Neusa Cardoso, who used to get up around four or four-thirty in the morning. This one time she went into her backyard and when she looked up in the sky she saw a red ball in the back yard of the house next door, about ten meters away from her and close to the ground.

"She was afraid but it didn't hurt her. When she called the people in the house, it disappeared. This was in March or April 1977."

CHOPPER COPS AND UFO GO ROUND AND ROUND

Two helicopter police officers on routine patrol had a close encounter with two UFOs that left one officer admitting it "scared hell out of me."

The UFOs were tracked on radar at the nearby municipal airport with one fleeing UFO from the chopper at about 200 MPH. During the encounter, one object and the copter flew circles around one another.

"It seemed to be playing games with us," said the chopper pilot, Patrolman Ronald K. Arey, then 39.

"There's no doubt in my mind that this was intelligently controlled. I can't say whether anybody was in it. I don't know… It evidently knew what I was doing because it appeared to me like it was trying to get on my tail and I was trying to get on its tail."

With Officer Arey was Patrolman Howard Douglas Dellinger, then 31, his observer in the Bell Jet Ranger 206B police chopper, which was named *Snoopy II*. They were on patrol over the city of Charlotte, North Carolina, on the night of December 27, 1977, when the encounter occurred.

"This was approximately five or six minutes before eleven," Arey said. "We were flying over Independence Boulevard on the east side of Charlotte. The dispatcher gave out a call to Ninth and College, a car being pursued by police officers.

"We turned to a northwesterly heading and headed toward Ninth and College. On the way, approximately over Hawthorne and Central Avenue, we observed what looked like two aircraft flying in formation. They were headed southeast at about two thousand feet.

"As we got close to them I observed that there were no navigational lights, no rotating beacons, no strobe lights or anything on the aircraft. I pointed them out to my partner and we went under them."

Arey, who was six-foot-three and a thirteen-year police veteran, had been flying for seven years and had been flying the police chopper for five. Before that, he had been an Army radar operator assigned to a Nike Hercules missile unit in California.

"We went on up to Ninth and College and it turned out there was nothing to the call," Arey continued. "So I turned back to the southeast toward the Coliseum to see who was flying out there with no navigational lights or anything.

0 0 0

UFO GETS ON CHOPPER'S TAIL

"Nobody is supposed to fly over the city at less than a thousand feet above the highest obstacle. The field elevation in Charlotte is 700 feet above sea level, so they would have to fly at at least 1,700 feet, just about where they were.

"And there were no navigational lights or anything. It kind of worried me if somebody's up there with us. We're out there on a mission and on a mission both of us have to look at the ground and you can't look for aircraft that close.

"As I got to the Coliseum, I didn't see anything. I went to the south of the Coliseum and circled to the left and headed back toward the north. As I made my turn, I observed two objects still flying in formation and still at about 1,800 to 2,000 feet.

"I started slowing down and climbing. I climbed to about 1,500 or 1,600 feet and was approximately 200 feet under them. As they went by, they passed on my left, so I automatically turned to the left."

"The one to my left made a left turn. That put him directly on my tail. The one that was furthest from me went up to about 4,000 or 5,000 feet in two or three seconds. I was trying to get around to see the other one and it seemed to keep circling me. It looked like it was playing games.

"No aircraft will turn as sharp as a helicopter, because you can do a pedal turn and you can spin the rear end of that thing right around. And that's what we were doing.

"He was approximately a hundred fifty to two hundred feet behind me and he had a larger circumference to go around. He had a lot more distance to travel than I did – and as soon as I could get a look at it, it was right back on my tail.

"I asked the tower, 'Have you got any targets on the scope out here?' And he says, 'Yeah, I've got two targets painting on the scope right there at the Coliseum.' As I was turning to the left I was talking to the tower, too.

"As I swung toward the tower, I flipped the landing light on, on the helicopter, and he told me, 'I have visual contact.' And the controller said 'There's one appears to be right behind you and the other one is heading towards Monroe.'

"I was circling to the left and it started circling to the left. We were just standing up there doing tailspins. I slowed my airspeed down to approximately twenty-five or thirty miles an hour and I was kicking the pedal, spinning the rear end around. As soon as I would spin it around, it seemed like it was right back in behind me!

"We did two or three 360-degree turns. It seemed like the thing was just playing games with me. It gives you a little bit of an eerie feeling. I mean, is this thing going to run into the back of me? I mean, we're close together!

BRIGHT ORANGE LIGHT

"So I kicked the right pedal and immediately flipped it back to the right – and that's when I got a good look at it. It paused, just for a second. It was a light... a bright orange-white or orange-yellow light.

"It appeared to be about twelve inches in diameter. It was not the type of light that penetrated, like an automobile headlight or a landing light on an aircraft. There was no beam to it. It just glowed and the light reflected up over it and down.

"The front portion was all I could see, because the light was only reflected on that part. It was an oval-shaped top, a silver-looking type object. It looked like it had ribs in it, like seams where it was put together.

"I was kind of flabbergasted. I said to Doug, 'What in the hell is that?' And he said, 'You've got me – let's get out of here.' The object immediately turned to an easterly or southeasterly direction, a ball of fire as big as your fist came out from underneath and dropped down, and the object headed off.

"I gave chase to the object. I pulled ninety to ninety-five percent torque on the chopper, which would put me up to about a hundred forty miles an hour. Top speed is one fifty. The object ran off and left me.

"It looked like it was two or three miles ahead of me. We were getting it pretty good down through there and all of a sudden the light went out and we couldn't see anything else."

During all this, Arey was in constant contact with the traffic control tower operator at Douglas Municipal Airport seven to nine miles west of the Coliseum.

"At my first observance to all this I told the control tower operator I was over the Coliseum and asked him if he had any targets painting on his screen in proximity to me," said Arey. "He stated that he had an aircraft that just went over that way, headed toward Albemarle. I observed that aircraft, a Cessna about five or six miles from me.

"The controller said he had two more targets there in proximity to me. He said one was headed in a south or southeasterly direction and the other was right there in proximity to me.

0 0 0

SCARED HELL OUT OF ME

"I told him we had something out there flying without any navigational lights or anything. He said, 'I'll follow it (on radar) and see if you can catch up with it.' We were unable to catch it. After we lost it, the control tower told me he had an aircraft south of me between South Park shopping Center and the Coliseum.

"We turned south and there was an object in the sky, the same thing we had sighted before. We headed towards it. It appeared to be two or three thousand feet high. "We got about a mile or a mile and a half and the light disappeared. Just went out. We could see nothing. I immediately came on the radio and asked the control tower operator, 'Do you still have the target on the scope?' And he says, 'No, I just dropped it.'"

Patrolman Dellinger, six-foot-two and a police officer for eight years, said that in the beginning he thought two aircraft were just coming across the sky. "I didn't pay too much attention to them. I'd been in this unit only two or three months. I just kept my eyes on them. They came on by and went over us and Ron turned the helicopter around.

"I said, 'What was that?' And Ron said, 'I don't know – we're going to find out.' He started getting close to them and one shot way up there about 4,000 feet. I was busy watching the other one. It was over on my side.

"It scared hell out of me. I didn't know what it was. I haven't flown that much and it just scared me. It was a light with ribs in it with sides coming down like the sides of a parachute. Ron kept trying to get in behind it and get it where we could put our spotlight on it to see what it was. Never could do that.

"I told Ron, 'There's some things you fool with and I don't think this is one or them.' That thing bothered me. I don't know what it was and I'm just not used to that stuff. I wanted him to get the hell out of there.

"It was a little bit scary. It makes you wonder. If it is something from outer space and hasn't bothered anybody and you start bothering them, and if they're intelligent enough to get down here, no telling what they could do to you."

Ray Bader, then one of two air traffic controllers for the Federal Aviation Administration on duty at Douglas Municipal Airport in Charlotte that night, said: "It was about ten fifty-five on the date in question that *Snoopy II*, the city helicopter, called in and asked if I had any targets in his vicinity. A target is a radar paint of an aircraft or object in the sky.

TWO TARGETS ON RADAR

"I said yes and tried to identify the one that I knew, which was a Cessna eastbound. I had a general idea where *Snoopy* was. He was over the Coliseum. And he said, 'No, no, there're two other ones.' And at that time I saw two other targets in the vicinity of the Coliseum. I saw three targets in the vicinity of the Coliseum and a Cessna eastbound. Two of the targets were very close to each other.

"I asked *Snoopy* to show his light towards the tower so I could get an idea where he was and see if I could visually see the other aircraft by using binoculars. *Snoopy* turned toward the tower and put his light on and another fellow in the tower and I were looking with binoculars to the east and we didn't see anything other than the light.

"A little later he (Arey) said he had lost the target he was following and was looking around for it and saw a light to the northeast of the Charlotte airport, which I identified as an inbound Eastern jet.

"He asked me if I saw anything else and I said yes I did, about a mile and a half south of your position. He turned around and proceeded down that way and he said he saw it again. And then he said he lost it.

"About twenty or thirty minutes later, the two policemen came to the control tower and we talked about what had happened and got other details, such as at one point he said the unknown climbed to 4,000 feet and was tracking southeast bound.

"At that time we had seen a target head southeast and then disappear from the screen about five to seven miles northwest of the Monroe Airport. When *Snoopy* said he had lost the second aircraft, we didn't see it any longer on the screen either."

Bader had been a control tower operator for four years at that time, and for years before that was a ground control approach controller at Cherry Point, North Carolina, Marine Corps base.

"This one object went off at about 200 miles an hour," said Bader. "This was approximately the same time Arey said one was just pulling away from him.

"I don't remember seeing *Snoopy* chase it. I remember seeing the targets all together. He might have chased it for a mile or two but that wouldn't give me a good return."

Bader said he did not know what the objects were. "At the time I didn't think of trying to contact anybody. I wasn't just watching *Snoopy*. I had other aircraft at the time.

ANOTHER WITNESS

"The other controller in the tower was Tom Carmody. He was busy with something else most of the time but he confirmed that he saw a target southeast bound when I did and he was looking through the binoculars trying to get visual contact."

Bader said neither the Cessna nor the Eastern jetliner would have been close enough to see the objects near *Snoopy*.

"The Cessna wasn't real close," said Bader. "He was either right over them or had already passed them when *Snoopy* started calling in. He was at 3,500 feet, so he was above and it would have been hard to see something like that. He was at least five miles further east and going away so he probably would not have seen them. The Eastern jet was still twenty miles out so he wouldn't have been able to see much, either.

Major Tom Ginn, then administrative assistant to the chief of police for the Charlotte Police Department, said in commenting on Officers Arey and Dellinger: "I'm sure that whatever these men have told you in reference to whatever the objects were that they saw that night, you can go ahead and print it because I have all the confidence in the world in them. I'm sure they're not the type of people that would make up things as far as something of this importance is concerned."

At least one other person is known to have seen something strange in the sky that evening. He is Eric Moore, then 22 and an announcer for radio station WRPL in Charlotte.

"It was around nine o'clock," Moore said. "I got gas across the street and as I was leaving I saw what looked like a light bulb hanging up in the sky. It looked a little strange. It didn't look like an airplane or anything. It was traveling pretty slow too, and it was relatively close.

"I buzzed down the road a little bit and the thing went right over the car and I could see something hanging down below it. It looked like it was transparent but it was not any kind of gas or vapor. It was solid.

"The thing went on over and was heading southeast, like it could have been following traffic or possibly power lines.

"I went on across Independence Boulevard and got over near Central Piedmont College, trying to keep it in sight. I had to stop at a few red lights and kept watching it. I got up to Central Piedmont and looked over and the thing had disappeared by then, and I saw another one over near the Coliseum. It wasn't moving at all, or didn't appear to be. I just took them to be a couple of weather balloons and didn't really follow them."

WORD LEAKS OUT

He described what he saw as "a bright, white light. It didn't appear to have any depth, just a glow. It was pretty large and appeared to be about the size of a silver dollar in the sky. Something definitely was hanging down.

"The glow from the light reflected off it. At first, I thought something has happened to the balloon or it might be some type of indicator or equipment. It was a grayish or transparent color. It was not shiny."

Although the sighting occurred on a Tuesday night, it wasn't until the following Saturday that the first story about it appeared in the Charlotte newspapers.

"I didn't tell anybody about this until I saw the Saturday morning paper," Moore said. "And Then I remembered and thought, 'Wow! I might have seen the same thing.'"

Officer Arey said he deliberately did not say anything about the objects over the police radio during the encounter. "All the newspapers in Charlotte monitor our frequency and the first thing I thought about was keeping my mouth shut. I told Doug, 'You say anything to anybody about this, I'll shoot you.'"

After talking with Bader at the tower, he and Dellinger returned to police headquarters to report to the duty officer in person.

"We didn't want anything to get out, to start with, so we came back and talked to the duty officer and told him exactly what we'd seen," said Arey. "He has to log everything that goes on. He puts it in his log.

"I was trying to keep it quiet. I didn't want it on the police radio. People think you're a bunch of kooks. They really will. And I know if we'd come back and landed, the whole roof of the police department would be full of reporters and I didn't want that.

"So we told the duty captain and, I don't know, it got out over the station. The next duty captain saw it. All the duty captains read it and the next thing we knew the newspapers had it."

The object was bigger than the chopper, Officer Dellinger said. "I would say it was about one and a half times as large as the helicopter. There was some kind of a shape above the light."

CIRCLE DANCE WAS "TOO LONG"

"You had the main light, the solid part, and then the glow around that. And then you could see in the glow and over the top of the glow a little bit that was like a funnel, like the sides of a parachute. It had ribs in the middle there and kind of a dome like over it."

Arey added: "The light itself appeared to be about twelve inches in diameter... It would have been much larger if we'd gotten up close to it, but you couldn't see the whole thing."

The two officers said the entire encounter, from the first moment they spotted the objects while answering a dispatcher's call to Ninth and College Streets until the last one disappeared, was about five minutes.

Dellinger estimated the close encounter with the object they circled with, lasted "twenty to thirty seconds."

"Long enough to do about two or three 360-degree turns," Arey said.

Too long," Dellinger added.

UFO REPORTS OFFICER ENCOUNTERS TWO UFOs

Waugh (undersheriff of Eber County in Colorado) said he had had several personal encounters with UFOs.

"One morning around two-thirty or three, a posse man and I were sitting down on the road and we saw a big orange ball of light coming up behind a house. I saw three little lights in what could be a cockpit, but you couldn't see anything else. It was moving fast.

"Another time, one came right down the road at me and it was car level, just like the lights on a car coming at me. And then it went down! This thing came at me right down the road and it scared me. Anytime a man says he doesn't get scared by anything is a damned fool or a liar. I was scared.

"I cut my motor and grabbed my rifle and jumped out of the car but the thing seemed to have gone down into the ground. I mean it vanished. There was a dip in the road but it was just a short ways in front of me. It went down and didn't show up again. I don't know what happened to it.

"What I had seen was just a big orange ball. That's what we'd see in the sky every time there was mutilation."

Although he grabbed his rifle, he said he wouldn't have shot at it. "I made up my mind to this – if I came across something I wasn't going to start shooting until I knew exactly what I was shooting at because if I did and they can kill a cow and we don't know how, my shotgun or rifle or .38 or whatever isn't going to be nothing, and I wasn't going to be stupid enough to shoot at them and get them mad at me.

"I used to tell people there's nothing to be afraid of. If they wanted to take people they would have taken them before they took cattle. I don't think, outside of the ranchers losing beef, it's anything to worry about unless they decide to start experimenting on humans.'

POLICEMAN GETS UFO IN HIS SIGHTS

A UFO that hovered over a golf course in Memphis, Tennessee was truly enormous, say two police officers who stood almost underneath it.

"It was about as long as a football field and fifty to seventy-five yards wide," said Patrolman Troy Todd. He and his partner, Patrolman Jerry Jeter, were definitely impressed.

"It was 300 to 500 meters above us and we could see the whole belly of the craft," Jeter said.

The two were members of the police department's Tactical Squad, men who are specially chosen for their coolness, intelligence, and special skills with weapons. Three other members of the squad saw a similar object earlier in the evening but at a greater distance.

"I believe what I saw was an unidentified flying object and I believe it was some aircraft not of this earth," said Todd, then 29.

The two men reported seeing the object hovering over a municipal golf course in the southern part of Memphis about three thirty in the morning of May 17, 1977. They got out of their unmarked police van and watched the object for two or three minutes.

As members of the Tactical Squad, they carried special weapons with them. Jeter took a rifle with a telescopic sight out of its case to get a better look at the craft. He said that as soon as he shouldered the rifle and pointed it at the object to look at it through the scope, the object shot off across the horizon in an instant.

It was an awesome sight and marked the end of a strange night for Todd, Jeter, and three other officers.

Four and a half hours earlier, three other members of the Tactical Squad – Patrolmen John Birdsong, Michael Davidson, and Forrest Bartlett – saw a triangular-shaped object lit up like "a Christmas tree" as it flew over a police substation in the northern part of the city.

TRIANGULAR OBJECT SPOTTED

Birdsong was going off duty at the time and the other two were just going on duty. The three said nothing to anybody at the time about their sighting.

However, later in the night when Jeter radioed the central dispatcher and said he and Todd had sighted a UFO, Davidson asked them by radio if it was triangular in shape and had multicolored lights.

Jeter replied yes. Until then, neither he nor Todd had said anything on the radio about the object's shape or lights and had given no other details. All five officers believe they saw the same object.

Of the two sightings, the one by Jeter and Todd was more spectacular. They had been driving an unmarked police van south on Interstate 240 in the city when Todd spotted something in the sky.

"I was driving and as we approached the Norris Road exit I observed to my left, which would have been to the east, a triangular-shaped series of lights over some high tension towers," said Todd.

"I really didn't know what I had seen. It was a long, triangular-shaped series of lights approximately thirty five to fifty feet above those towers and it tapered down to a narrow point."

He asked Jeter if he had seen it, but Jeter said no.

"I couldn't figure out exactly what it was so we went underneath Alcy Road and turned around on the median and went back up to the same location," said Todd, then an eight-year veteran.

"Both Jeter and I looked over those high-tension wires and we couldn't see anything at all. So we proceeded northbound on the expressway to South Parkway, turned around and came south, and this time we both observed it approximately 500 feet above the Pine Hill Golf Course, which would have been to the west off the expressway.

"This was approximately in the same line where I had a seen it before but it was at a greater height and it was on the other side of the expressway. So I drove the van up onto the Norris Road exit, we stopped and got out and watched it for two or three minutes.

"It was a triangular-shaped object with white, red, and green lights on it with a white glow about the silhouette itself."

Definitely Not a Helicopter

Jeter, a police officer for nine years, said that at first Todd thought he'd spotted a helicopter hovering over the power towers.

"When we both saw it he said, 'There it is again!' and I said, 'Well, it's not a helicopter.' It was elongated and looked like a triangular type shape. This object made its way over to the golf course and turned and was just hovering or standing still over the golf course.

"We pulled up this incline and got out and were looking at this object. In my estimation it was 300 to 500 meters high and we were at a slight angle from it, not directly under it but a real slight angle and we could see the whole belly of the craft.

"It had red and green lights flashing alternately on it and it looked like what were either portholes or real dim lights along the side of the craft. I really couldn't tell because they were so dim but it lit up the craft so you could see it, and to me it looked like a metallic craft.

"We had a telescopic rifle sight in the van and I was going to get it out and look at it. By the time I got it out of the case and everything and got it up to my shoulder, this craft turned slightly, two red lights came on, on the rear, and it just shot out over the horizon.

"This thing moved at such a speed it was unbelievable. It shot out of sight."

Todd said that when Jeter shouldered the rifle, the object "began to move off in a northerly direction at a reasonably slow speed. There was no sound made from the object. The white and green lights went off. They were no longer visible to us, but the glow was still visible around the silhouette.

"Then two red lights came on, on the rear of it. Whether they were lights or not, I'm not sure but when those two red lights came on, it sped out at a tremendous rate of speed and disappeared over the horizon in just a second to a second and a half. We were barely able to keep it in our eyesight.

"That night the weather conditions were extremely clear. Visibility was fifteen to twenty miles, I would say, because we were at the top of the expressway looking north."

NOTHING ON RADAR

Jeter got on the radio to the central dispatcher. "Todd didn't want to call. He said they'll think we're crazy. I said, what the hell, let's call. I don't give a damn. So I called the dispatcher and said how about checking with the air control tower (at Memphis International Airport) and see if they have any craft in this area.

"He (the traffic controller) checked and said no, they didn't show anything on radar. He said, 'Why?' and I said, 'Well, we saw what we figured to be a UFO' and everybody started coming on the air," Jeter said, laughing.

"And the catcalls started," added Todd.

Jeter said the dispatcher told him to switch to Channel Six so Patrolmen Davidson and Bartlett could talk to them.

'We didn't say what shape it was or anything," Jeter said, "and they came on and said was this object triangular or pyramidal in shape and we said, yes it was. They said they were standing out on the parking lot at the substation and it came streaking over at twenty three hundred hours."

Both Todd and Jeter said the craft made no noise as it hovered above the golf course nor when it moved off.

"It was huge," said Jeter. 'I would say a hundred meters in length. Tremendous. We went back and looked at those towers after it was over and those towers are seventy-five meters apart. This thing was overlapping them."

Todd described his initial sighting and said, 'It was sitting with the nose off one side of one tower and the tail off the side of the other.

"My first sighting of it was a side view. It was more of a delta-wing shape. It had a flat bottom with a taper from the top of a flat back which I would say was thirty five to fifty feet high and it tapered down to a small point.

"When we observed it the second time, when we both observed it, we were looking at it from the bottom and it was triangular shaped. It was a silvery, gun metal color."

KIND OF BAMBOOZLED

When asked what he thought when he saw the object, Todd replied: "We were kind of bamboozled but in my opinion it was definitely a flying aircraft from someplace. It was something I had never seen before and it was of tremendous size.

"Something of that size that could hover the way it was would have to make some type of noise. I don't know if the United States has an aircraft that can hover without making noise but I don't believe so.

"When I made the initial sighting it was more of confusion and wonder at what I had actually seen. And then on my second sighting and seeing it cross the horizon like it did, I knew what it was.

"In my opinion I believe what I saw was an unidentified flying object and I believe it was some aircraft not of this earth."

All five men worked out of the North Precinct on Old Allen Road about fifteen miles northeast of the golf course. It was in the substation's parking lot where Patrolmen Birdsong, Davidson, and Bartlett spotted the object earlier in the night.

"We were sitting in the parking lot on the west side of the substation talking," said Birdsong. He and Davidson were facing north and Bartlett, sitting on the trunk of a car, was facing them.

"I looked up and saw an object going overhead and told Davidson, 'Look, there goes a flying saucer,'" said Birdsong. "I didn't know what it was and Davidson looked up and we tried to get Bartlett to look around. He thought we were just kidding.

"He wouldn't look at first and finally he turned around and looked and said, 'It looks like a flying Christmas tree.' It was shaped like a triangle and it had lights all around it and underneath it. It was traveling at a pretty good speed."

Bartlett said that when he did look around he saw "a triangular-shaped object just going by. The point of it was to the front and there were multicolored lights. They were a soft yellow to a bright orange with some greenish tint.

HIGH FLYING OBJECT

"We Just laughed and wondered what it was. Nobody had any real comment or anything because we heard no sound or anything."

Some time later, Birdsong and Davidson heard Jeter and Todd say on the radio that they'd seen a UFO. "We got them to switch to Channel six so we could talk to them and Davidson asked them if it was a triangular-shaped object and had multicolored lights, and they said. 'Check.' So then we knew right off it was the same object we had seen earlier."

The object made no noise, Davidson said. "It was pretty high up. The lights were more or less like a Christmas tree. It had lights around it and in the center also, different colors. Green, white, and yellow were the ones I remember distinctly. They were separate, individual lights. They didn't blend into each other.

"We just shrugged it off. We thought it was something from the naval air station."

A spokesman at the Millington Naval Air Station, located eight miles north of the police substation, said no craft similar to the one the men described was based there. He said the radar at the station is shut down at eleven o'clock each night and would not have picked up anything at the time the officers spotted the UFO.

Memphis Police Capt. Paul J. Acerra, who was the duty officer the night Jeter and Todd reported spotting the UFO, said: "These officers are all mature men with good judgment. To get into the Tactical unit you have to be above average. All of them are responsible citizens. They would not make up anything like this. None of them."

Ed Becton, a supervisor in the Federal Aviation Authority air traffic control tower at the Memphis International Airport, said: "The next day we had calls from maybe fifty different reporters, radios, and TV stations about this. We checked with all the air traffic controllers on duty at the time and they had nothing on radar in the area of the golf course and they saw nothing visually."

POLICE DOG IS
KILLED BY A UFO

A watchdog trying to protect his rancher owner was no match for a glowing UFO, fiercely charging the UFO as it hovered near them. The dog initially survived the encounter but died two days later. His master was burned on one arm.

The incident was one of a number of UFO sightings that occurred in northwestern Uruguay in early 1977, a time when several UFO waves and numerous sightings were reported around the world. In Uruguay, entire cities were blacked out as UFOs hovered over high-tension power lines.

The rancher was Angel Maria Tonna, then 52, who owned 3,000 acres of rolling farmland with more than 700 head of cattle and numerous sheep. The ranch is located fifteen kilometers south of Salto, then a city of 40,000 inhabitants on the Uruguay River.

Tonna and fifteen others – his wife, their two sons, 19 and 22, and daughter, 15, and his eleven farmhands – saw UFOs about a dozen times in February and March that year. The most serious incident occurred about four o'clock the morning of February 18 as Tonna and his foreman, Juan Manuel Fernandez, were herding about eighty cows into a barn to be milked.

"When I get up in the morning, I usually turn the generator on, so I turned the generator on that morning and there were about twenty lights on around the barn and other buildings," Tonna said. "I was bringing the cows in to be milked and suddenly, about ten minutes after four, all the lights went off.

THOUGHT BARN WAS BURNING

"A bright light appeared on the far end of the barn from me and I could see the barn's shadow. I thought it was a short circuit. I keep hay in that end of the barn for the cows and I thought the barn was burning. I jumped over the fence and ran toward the barn.

"Topo was with me. He's a watchdog and he always used to walk with me wherever I went around the farm in the mornings.

"Then I heard a noise, and the next thing I saw was a 'fire' disc, like two plates facing each other, on the other side of the barn. I stood there not knowing what to do. My foreman told me the cows were running away. The cows were going crazy, running everywhere, and all the dogs started barking.

"The object began to move. It broke the branches of a tree near the barn and moved across the barnyard to my right and then hovered over some trees about a hundred meters south of the barn. It moved across the barnyard with a rocking motion."

Tonna held one hand out with fingers spread horizontally and tipped it from side to side. The object sat about twenty meters above the trees for a moment, then moved to Tonna's right and went another seventy-five meters or so. At that point, it moved down closer to the ground and halted directly above a concrete bath that cows are forced to walk through to disinfect them.

By this time Tonna and Topo, a 3-year-old black and brown police dog, weighing more than sixty pounds, had run back to the side of the barnyard where they'd started, and climbed back over the fence again. They walked a few feet toward the UFO, which was now glowing bright orange.

A few seconds later, it made another right turn and drifted slowly toward them before finally coming to a stop about six meters above the ground and next to a water tank.

Dog Charges UFO

"It was shining with a very bright light and lit up the whole barnyard," Tonna said. "Topo ran toward the object to attack it, but suddenly, he stopped on a little mound, sat down and began howling."

Topo was within five meters of the object and sat looking up at it. "The object was about twenty meters from me," Tonna said. "I saw six beams of light on it in the shape of small wings, like lightning, three on each side. When the object turned toward me it felt like electric shocks went all over my body and a very intensive heat hit me. I put my arm up over my face to protect my eyes.

"I was scared. For some reason I couldn't move. I felt attracted to the light. I don't know if I couldn't move or didn't want to."

After several minutes, the object began moving away, turning from bright orange to red.

"When it moved away, it increased its speed as it was turning red and when it got to the forest (about one kilometer to the south), it disappeared. After the object left, the generator started working again but it wasn't producing electricity because the wires were burned out."

The incident lasted about ten minutes. Tonna's 19-year-old son, Túlio, then a university student in Salto, had watched the incident from the house. A few farmhands had awakened to start their workday but saw only a bright light in the area.

"Topo didn't eat anything after that," Tonna said. "He walked around as he normally would but he wouldn't eat or drink anything. He stayed in the house all day, which wasn't normal. It was like with a sad feeling."

DISTURBING AUTOPSY REPORT

On the morning of the third day after the UFO incident, Topo's body was found on the very same mound where he had sat howling at the UFO. Tonna said a veterinarian who teaches at the North University in Salto performed an autopsy at the ranch. Túlio Tonna said he and three other second-year veterinary students assisted him.

Túlio would not identify the veterinarian and said the professor refused to discuss the case. The country was then under a military dictatorship and people were afraid of losing their jobs if they offended the government. However, Túlio said the veterinarian allowed him to make a copy of the autopsy report. It said in part:

"The hair along the animal's spine was sticky but completely hard. The fat under the skin was found on the outside. The fat is normally solid, so to get to the outside it had to be melted and come through the pores. Once it was outside it solidified again. The animal was exposed to a very high temperature that can't be reached naturally by the dog.

"All the blood vessels had been bleeding very much and all the capillaries were broken. The rupture of the blood vessels was caused by an increase in temperature that couldn't be natural. The liver, normally dark and red, was completely yellow, caused by a high fever.

"All the blood vessels were yellow too. With all the blood vessels broken, the animal started bleeding inside and lost so much blood that 48 hours later the amount of blood he had circulated was insufficient and he died of a heart attack.

"When we took the skin off the dog, we didn't see any marks. He didn't have any bruises or anything... nor was the hair burned. The conclusion was that something very hot had caused this."

The underside of Angel Tonna's right arm began hurting the morning after the UFO incident. He had turned that side toward the UFO when he put his arm up to protect his eyes. Several days later, Dr. Bruning Herrara, a Salto physician and a friend, stopped at the Tonna ranch for a personal visit.

RADIATION BURN?

"When I first went to Mr. Tonna's house, I didn't know anything about the incident," Dr. Herrara told us later in a phone interview. "I talked to him and he said he wasn't feeling very well and we started talking about the incident. What I saw on Mr. Tonna's arm was an irritation. His arm was completely red.

"My first conclusion was that the skin irritation was due to radiation caused by an extremely bright light. I didn't find any other irritation on any other part of his body.

"I recommended that Mr. Tonna have a special examination to see if he had been exposed to radiation but he refused to do it. I don't know why. I didn't want to prescribe any kind of medicine for Mr. Tonna because I first wanted to know if he had been exposed to any kind of radiation... I didn't see him after that."

Tonna would have had to go to Montevideo, more than 300 kilometers away, for the examination and didn't want to take the time. He doctored himself with home remedies.

During that period of time, Tonna and his farmhands found at least a dozen dark green circles in pastures some distance from the house and farm buildings. Most measured about ten meters across, while several were nearly sixty meters across.

Showing us one ten-meter circle about three kilometers from the house, Tonna commented: "When we found it, the grass was burned, completely dead. Some time later, we found mushrooms growing on the outer edge and then the grass grew dark green."

He also found three circular impressions forming a triangle in the center of the ring, the impressions being about three meters apart. He also pointed out that the small rocks in the area were darker on the top than on the sides and bottoms, and appeared to have been burned.

CURIOUS TREE DAMAGE

In addition to the circles, two tall, healthy trees in a stand of eucalyptus trees planted ten years earlier as a wind break, were found uprooted and pushed to the ground one morning. "A worker found the trees," Tonna said as he showed us the two fallen trees. "I couldn't believe it because there wasn't any storm or any strong winds or anything that night."

Curiously, both trees were in the outside row on the east side of the grove, which was about a thousand meters long and sixty meters wide. Each tree was the eighth tree from the end, one from the north

end and one from the south end, and each had been pushed in toward the center of the grove. Each was leaning at about a forty-five-degree angle against other trees inside the grove.

Numerous sightings were reported in Salto and the city of Paysandu, about a hundred kilometers to the south. There were more than twenty sightings in Tonna's neighborhood alone. Mario Rodriguez, then an electronics engineer and a UFO investigator from Montevideo, interviewed about twenty other witnesses in the Salto area, *but learned there had been many more witnesses, hundreds if not thousands.* Blackouts occurred simultaneously in the cities of Salto, Paysandu, and Young, and UFOs were seen over high-tension towers during the blackouts.

On Mario's first visit to Salto on February 27, Police Officer Hector Lopez drove him around the area to talk to people who had reported seeing UFOs. Lopez was then in charge of the police station at Parada Dayman, several kilometers from the Tonna home, and was one of several policemen who saw a brilliant UFO the night of February 22.

Lopez said he was sitting outside the police station that evening when he saw what he first thought was a flash of lightning. But the light continued, getting brighter and brighter. "It was so bright it lit up the area like daylight," Lopez said. "The light was so bright I could have seen a pin on the ground."

HORSEBACK SEARCH

He called the other policemen to come outside. Several climbed to the roof of the station but could see little more than what the men on the ground were seeing. Lopez then phoned police in Salto and Paysandu and learned they were experiencing a blackout at the same time, as was the small town of Young, southeast of Paysandu.

A short time later, the object seemed to fall apart, Lopez said. The next day he and several other officers on horseback searched the power lines for several miles in both directions. "There was nothing on the towers, nothing on the ground, no burned grass, nothing. I was very surprised. I have no explanation for this phenomenon. The light was seen not only in Salto but also in Paysandu... Almost everybody in Salto and Paysandu saw the light."

Lopez said the Paysandu police had also seen the light and had filed a report on it.

I first learned about the UFO wave and the Tonna case two months later, in April, when I first met Mario Rodriguez at an international UFO conference in Acapulco, Mexico. He told me about the many sightings in Uruguay. In July, after working for five days on a story in Torreon and Guadalajara, Mexico, I flew directly to Montevideo.

Mario came to my hotel, the Victoria Plaza, the evening I arrived and we made arrangements as I finished dinner. The next day Mario and an interpreter, Juan Manuel, and I flew the 300 kilometers or so to Salto on a small commuter plane flown by military pilots, the airline then being under control of the military.

This was my first trip to South America and my introduction to some of the customs of that continent. We arrived in Salto in late afternoon and I was hungry. I was astonished to find the restaurants closed. It was about six o'clock and I couldn't believe we were too late to eat. We weren't. I was as equally astonished to learn that many Uruguayans eat dinner late in the evening, and that most restaurants didn't open before eight.

(Two years later, I was to see an entire family with small children eating dinner in a restaurant around midnight in the small city of Malargue in western Argentina. By then, I was no longer surprised.)

THREE-KILOMETER AREA LIGHTS UP

The winter weather in Uruguay was cold and damp and, on Mario's advice, I bought a pair of rubber boots in Salto for the visit to Tonna's ranch. They came in very handy the next day when we waded through the deep mud and manure in Tonna's barnyard as he told us his story and pointed out where things happened. One man who had joined us from Salto wasn't as fortunate and lost his shoes in the muddy mess.

We spent the better part of a day interviewing Angel Tonna and his son Túlio and walking around the ranch, inspecting the curious circles and the two trees that appeared to have been pushed down in the Eucalyptus grove. The following day, we sought out other witnesses in Salto and towns in Tonna's neighborhood.

We talked to a couple who saw a UFO the same night that Officer Lopez and the other policemen did. They were Elida Gimenez, 56, who was in charge of the telephone exchange at Parada Dayman, and her husband, Angel Gimenez, 62. The phone exchange office was near the police station.

"At ten-ten in the evening, I heard a loud noise," Mrs. Gimenez said. "I went outside and saw a UFO over a high-tension tower. It was shining a very brilliant light and it lit up an area about three kilometers around. This tower is on Mr. Tonna's farm about three kilometers from here. It lit up the school and the police station too. All the radios went dead. The police saw it too.

"My husband climbed a pole and he was looking there and he heard a strange, funny noise, like when you touch two wires together.

The light had some blue in it, but after a while it started changing to orange and then bright red. The size of the object seemed to decrease and after that it disappeared.

"We thought it was a short circuit in one of the towers and I called the electric power company and they said there was a blackout in Salto."

UFO Seen During Blackout

A UFO organization in Salto investigated the series of sightings and one of its members, Alberto Ghizzoni, then 42, told me:

"Many of the people of the city have seen the phenomenon. There have been many blackouts. On the night of March 24 and 25, a blackout lasted for half an hour. When it started, everybody went out of their houses and they saw a disc-shaped object going from south to north. It remained in the air and got higher and higher until it looked like a star with a reddish color.

"The UFO stopped over the northwestern part of the city. After a while, it disappeared without moving, just faded out. The moment it disappeared, the lights began coming on again. The power and light company never gave any explanations. We interviewed an employee we know and he told us he was ordered to say that there was failure in the plant, but he was absolutely sure there was nothing wrong there."

Instead of flying back to Montevideo, we reserved seats on an overnight bus that allowed us to sleep on the way there, passing through Paysandu and many small towns enroute.

Angel Tonna's health deteriorated later that year but eventually he recovered. The case attracted international attention, and in the next year or two, reporters and UFO investigators from as far away as Russia visited the Tonna ranch.

About three years later, UFO investigators in nearby Rosário, Argentina, told me they had heard that a cult-like group had grown up around Tonna, shielding him from outsiders and making it difficult to see him anymore. However, I was never able to confirm this.

A Mistake...

Bob Pratt wrote:

A variation of this report was published in the April 1978 issue of the *MUFON UFO Journal* under another byline, [we are changing this name for this book], even though I wrote it. Because I was working for

the *National Enquirer* – which did not use the story for reasons that I no longer remember – I could not use my own name. I believed the story should be told and MUFON director Walt Andrus was happy to have it for the *Journal*. Since Miguel had been so helpful to me, I put his name on it – without asking him, unfortunately. I thought he would be pleased since he had been MUFON's representative in Uruguay for about a year. Instead, he was very upset when he learned about it. As I said earlier, at that time Uruguay was under a military dictatorship. It was in many ways a very poor country and nearly everybody needed two jobs to earn a living. Miguel, even though he had a degree in electronic engineering, supported his family by repairing television sets. Virtually everyone who worked for the government was afraid to talk about UFOs, or almost any other matter, for fear of losing his or her job. This included the Salto power company employees and the veterinary professor, none of whom would talk to us. Miguel himself, even though he didn't work for the government, was worried about what might happen to him if the government learned about the *MUFON UFO Journal* article. Fortunately, nothing did happen to him because of it, but a year or so later he and his family moved to Miami, Florida, where they now live. Uruguay has long since returned to civilian rule.

...And A Dissent

Dr. Willy Smith, author of the UNICAT catalog of UFO cases, strongly disagrees with me about what happened in this case. He says no autopsy was ever done on the dog.

Willy, a native of Uruguay who has spent most of his adult life in the United States as a physics professor, never visited the Tonna ranch or personally investigated the case. However, he formed his conclusions based on information given to him by researchers in Montevideo not associated with Mario Rodriguez.

Mario impressed me as an intelligent, thorough, and competent investigator not given to exaggeration. He remains convinced that the case is a valid one. I put my faith in Mario and my own interviews with the Tonnas and other witnesses.

Willy and I agreed to disagree. I first met him in the early 1980s when he lived in Longwood, Florida near Orlando and Dr. J. Allen Hynek, with whom I had worked for more than eight years, was visiting him. Dr. Hynek died in 1986.

(A similar version of this story was published in the August and September 1998 issues of the *MUFON UFO Journal*)

0 0 0

THE "VARGINHA ET CASE"

On the night of January 13, 1996, the North American Aerospace Defense Command reportedly notified Brazilian authorities that it had tracked a number of UFOs over the western hemisphere that night and one or more had come down near the city of Varginha in the state of Minas Gerais.

Brazilian authorities were quickly notified and they immediately alerted Army units near Varginha (*Var-ZJEEN-yuh*).

It was the beginning of one of the most intriguing events in UFO history, the "Varginha ET Case." Civilian investigators believe that over the next several weeks, at least two, and perhaps as many as six, alien creatures were captured or killed and turned over to American authorities, and that a UFO may have crashed.

Eyewitnesses described the creatures as humanoid and three to four feet tall. They had dark brown, hairless skin that was very oily, big triangular heads with three short "horns" on top, and huge red eyes that were vertically oval. The arms were long and thin, the legs short and thin. They had no obvious noses or ears and only slits for mouths. The creatures weren't wearing clothing and no sex organs were visible. They had unusually large veins growing out of their necks and running down their shoulders, arms, chest and back, making them look like weight lifters.

The "Varginha case" is a complicated one involving a series of incidents that apparently began on Saturday, January 13, but did not come to public attention until more than a week later after three young women spotted one of the creatures in a vacant lot. The young women had just finished helping a woman get ready to move to a new home on Saturday, January 20 and were walking to their own homes. Around three o'clock in the afternoon, they were passing through the Jardim Andere district of Varginha.

"We decided to take a short cut through a vacant lot," said Liliane da Silva, then 16, who was with her sister Valquíria, 14, and a friend, Kátia Xavier, 22.

Kátia was a maid for the woman who was moving, and the sisters, still in school, were helping her pack household goods. The three were walking to their homes in the Santana neighborhood just north of Jardim Andere.

The short cut took them on a narrow path through the vacant lot, which was then filled with tall grass and weeds. On their left was an empty cinder block building. When they were about fifty feet into the lot, something caught Liliane's attention.

"Look at that!" she cried. About twenty feet away was a strange creature squatting next to the building with its left side to them. (The yellow spot in the photo shows where the creature was crouching; note the same white paint mark on the wall.)

The creature's left arm was between its legs and the right was next to the building. Its feet were hidden in the grass, and the girls never saw the hands or feet.

"It had oily brown skin with big eyes and three 'horns' on its head," Liliane said.

The huge veins running down its neck into the shoulders reminded Valquíria of "a big, soft bull's heart. We thought it was the Devil."

To Kátia, who was married and had three children, it was "not a human or an animal, nothing like a monkey or anteater. We got a good look at the creature."

They found it repulsive, but the huge red eyes and the "horns" were what disturbed them most. They stared for a stunned few seconds, then screamed and recoiled in fright.

The creature turned its head and looked at them, seemed almost frightened and crouched a bit lower, perhaps trying to hide from them. The women fled back to the street behind them, turned right and ran away as fast as they could. They didn't stop until they reached the Silva home more than twenty blocks away.

After they calmed down about twenty minutes later, Kátia and the girls' mother, Luiza, asked a neighbor to drive them back to the vacant lot. By the time they got there, the creature was gone, Kátia said, "but we could see the grass mashed down and we could smell sulfur or ammonia." (In the photo are, from left, Bob Pratt, Liliane, Kátia in yellow pants, unidentified boys, and Valquíria in blue shorts.)

News of the incident spread quickly throughout the neighborhood and about ten-thirty the next morning reached the ears of Varginha's leading UFO investigator, Ubirajara Franco Rodrigues. He was then 42 and lived less than a mile from where the women saw the creature.

He got a phone call from a shop owner who had heard that "some girls had seen a weird animal, like a little monster."

The report was interesting, but it meant nothing to Ubirajara, a lawyer and university professor who has been investigating UFOs in the Varginha area since the 1970s. By evening, though, he had heard more rumors and then began trying to find out what had happened.

A friend named Sergio, who worked at a TV station, helped him and it took them several days to identify and locate Kátia and the sisters. These were days in which confusing and seemingly contradictory rumors were flying all over the city.

WOMEN CRY AS THEY TELL THEIR STORY

"Some people were saying a creature had been captured by Military Police and taken to Regional Hospital, that it had a big belly, seemed to be pregnant and made a noise like it was crying," Ubirajara said.

"We talked to a boy who said he saw the capture but his words didn't make any sense. He was too childish and very confused."

They tracked down a woman who also supposedly had seen the capture "but she ran away the moment we approached her. Her husband tried to convince her to talk to us but she refused."

When Ubirajara finally talked to the three women, they were still quite emotional about what happened. All three cried as they told their story.

In the following days he questioned them several more times and each time they related the same details without variation, bursting into tears the first several times. He became convinced they were telling the truth.

The rumors continued. A nurse reluctantly told Ubirajara that a section of Regional Hospital had been blocked off for some hours the night of January 20, with access being denied to patients, visitors, and even employees. Soldiers and Army vehicles had been parked outside, and unidentified physicians from other cities had come to the hospital.

On Monday the 22nd, all hospital employees were called together and told that everything that had happened that weekend was to be ignored because "it was just a training exercise for doctors and military personnel."

Then they were told that if anyone ("especially that lawyer, Ubirajara") should inquire about it, they were to deny everything.

The creature was reportedly transferred from Regional Hospital to Humanitas Hospital, which is much smaller and is in a more secluded location. More troops were seen there.

POLICE COLONEL TURNS MUM

One report said the creature, apparently dead, was seen lying in an open box propped up by two sawhorses in the Humanitas Hospital's walled-in parking lot. Fifteen people – military men, doctors and others – were said to have stood around the box, watching as one of the doctors used tweezers to pull a long, thin black tongue out of the creature's mouth.

Rumors abounded, even in schoolyards. One youngster was heard saying: "My daddy told me about the ET and said everything is true and he has seen a film but this is very dangerous and you cannot tell anyone."

Ubirajara checked around and learned that a relative of the child's father worked at a nearby Army base and was under house arrest at the base.

Ubirajara went to Military Police headquarters and talked to the commander, a lieutenant colonel. When Ubirajara explained why he was there, the colonel said he knew nothing about any creature but offered to check it out. Ubirajara phoned repeatedly over the next few days but was never able to reach the man again.

That was when Ubirajara began to believe something unusual really had taken place and that officials were hiding it. He became certain a day or so later when a friend talked with a policewoman who had been on duty on Saturday, January 20.

She said the police received a number of phone calls that morning through the emergency number from people "saying they saw a little monster. But we thought they were kidding and didn't pay any attention to them."

For nearly a month, the investigation proceeded in the belief that only one incident had occurred – that the three women had seen a creature which was later captured – and that for unknown reasons the authorities were trying to hush it up.

INVESTIGATORS JOIN FORCES

What was difficult to understand was that some of the rumors said the creature had been captured in the morning of January 20 BEFORE the three young women saw it in the afternoon.

The investigation entered a new phase in mid-February when Vitório Pacaccini joined the investigation. Pacaccini, who lived a hundred and ninety miles away in the state capital, Belo Horizonte, did not know Ubirajara at the time. He had learned about the case only on Sunday, February 11, when he read a newspaper story about the three women and the creature.

Pacaccini, then 32, had been a member of CICOANI, a UFO organization in Belo Horizonte, for eighteen years. At a special meeting two nights later, the members discussed the Varginha report, decided to investigate and chose Pacaccini to go to Varginha.

0 0 0

This was a practical choice for several reasons. First, his job as an import-export consultant had no set hours and allowed him considerable free time. Secondly, he had grown up in Três Corações, a city just fifteen miles east of Varginha. Furthermore, he had already made plans to go to Três Corações, where his widowed mother still lives, for the annual Carnaval festivities at the end of the week.

Três Corações plays a significant role in the case. ESA (*Escola de Sargentos das Armas*, or the Army's school for sergeants), the area's largest Army base, is located there and personnel from the base are believed to have taken a major role in the hunt for and capture of the creatures.

The day after the CICOANI meeting, February 14th, Pacaccini drove to Três Corações, phoned Ubirajara to introduce himself and set up a meeting for the following day.

INFORMANT CLARIFIES SITUATION

In an extraordinary coincidence, shortly after arriving at his mother's home, Pacaccini got a phone call from a friend saying a man who knew about the capture of the creature would be willing to talk to him.

The three met late that night in a secluded area, where the man described how four firemen had captured the creature on the MORNING of January 20 and took it to ESA.

The informant's story helped clear up the confusing rumors. Only then did Ubirajara and Pacaccini realize there had been two creatures, one captured in the morning and taken to ESA and one seen by the three women, which may have been caught later that day and taken to the Regional Hospital.

Eventually, Ubirajara and Pacaccini came to believe the authorities had captured or killed at least four other creatures and possibly as many as six.

Originally, Pacaccini had intended to conduct his own investigation, but after meeting with Ubirajara and exchanging information with him, the two agreed to work together.

Over the next six months or so, Pacaccini was able to make frequent trips to Varginha from Belo Horizonte. This took much of the burden off Ubirajara, who had a busy law practice and taught two nights a week at a university where he was a law professor and a lecturer in philosophy.

The two weren't working blind. The case quickly attracted the attention of newspapers, radio, and TV stations and began to get considerable publicity, both locally and nationally. Ubirajara received hundreds of phone calls, many from people who knew something about what had happened, or knew someone who knew someone who…

They checked out every rumor and report, and tracked down every witness or potential witness.

All Involved Identified

Among other things, they heard about a farm couple who saw a UFO very early on the morning of January 20 (true); a woman who saw a creature at the city's zoo (true); a portable radar station that was trucked in from southern Brazil (unconfirmed); a motorist who saw a creature weeks later (true); and a military man who told a friend he had helped capture "an ET" (unconfirmed).

There were also rumors about another military person whose uniform got so "oily" in capturing a creature that his wife burned his clothing (unconfirmed); the mysterious death of a policeman who had captured one creature (true); and the puzzling deaths of five animals at the zoo (true).

Ubirajara and Pacaccini eventually were able to talk to twenty-five firsthand witnesses – civilians, Military Policemen, Army personnel, doctors, and others. They also learned the identities of nearly every military person involved with the creatures in any way.

At the same time, investigators in other cities were also helping, mainly by checking rumors that on January 23 several creatures had been convoyed to the renowned University of Campinas, where an autopsy was performed on one creature. The university is located in Campinas, a city more than 200 miles south.

This story is based mainly on visits we made to Varginha in March 1996, just two months after most of these events took place, and again in August 1997. We spent four days there the first time, talking with Ubirajara and Pacaccini, before very much was known, and six days the second visit.

We were able to interview the three young women involved, Liliane on both visits, and another witness, a jogger whose testimony is related later.

In addition, we were able to visit several sites where things occurred. This included the then-vacant lot where the girls saw a creature, a steep embankment several blocks away where another creature was seen, the woods where that creature was captured, and a huge pasture beside it where armed soldiers were seen searching for something. The lot is no longer vacant and several houses have been built there.

Only Ubirajara was available the second time we went to Varginha, Pacaccini being elsewhere in the state. Ubirajara's time was limited because of his law practice and his teaching. In addition, he was leading a UFO conference in a nearby city the last four days of our visit.

In the beginning Ubirajara told us: "As an attorney, if I was in a court of law and had to prove that the firemen had captured an alien from another planet – with proof coming from an accredited place like the University of Campinas which would issue an official notice that said, 'One dead alien blah, blah, blah, of this blood type or other' – we have not been able to get that.

"We believe such reports exist and that this actually happened. I can prove – with testimony and witnesses, and we HAVE the witnesses – that these things occurred, but we don't have any official reports. A creature was captured, but where it came from we can't prove without analysis."

Following are some of the things we learned. In all instances, the creatures were much like the one described by the three young women.

THE SETTING

Most of these events took place in or near Varginha. It is a lively, busy city of about a hundred and twenty thousand people in the south of Minas Gerais, a state nearly as large as Texas. Minas has thousands of cities, towns and villages, nearly twenty million people, many ore-rich mines and other natural resources, and lots of industries, including auto manufacturing plants.

Varginha is almost equidistant from Brazil's three largest cities – about 200 miles north of São Paulo, 200 miles northwest of Rio de Janeiro and nearly 200 miles south of Belo Horizonte. It has a number of industries, including multinational corporations (American, Canadian, English, and French), and is a leading coffee exporting center. It has three hospitals, four universities and vocational-technical training centers, four daily newspapers, four radio stations, and three TV stations.

Much of the state of Minas Gerais is mountainous. Varginha is 3,100 feet above sea level and is spread out over a number of hills. Contrary to some Internet reports about the case, there are no jungles or predatory wild animals within at least a thousand miles. The countryside is lush and green, with much of it devoted to growing coffee.

THE MAIN CAPTURE SITE:

Many of the main incidents in the case occurred in or near a big patch of woods that separates the Jardim Andere and Santana neighborhoods. Both districts are about a mile and a half east of downtown. The woods run a bit more than a mile north and south and are up to 300 yards wide east and west. A small stream runs through the woods.

An east-west street connecting Jardim Andere and Santana cuts through the middle of the woods, and a single set of railroad tracks runs north-south through the area, skirting the upper edge of the woods on the Jardim Andere side.

A number of well-worn paths run through the woods and a huge adjoining pasture. People going to and from Jardim Andere and Santana use them regularly.

The three young women who saw the creature had planned to go through these woods as they took a short cut home. They were walking downhill when they entered the vacant lot, which is three blocks above the railroad tracks and the woods.

NORAD, JANUARY 13

Pacaccini – who owns a business arranging for the shipment of goods into and out of Brazil in seagoing cargo containers and also manages his family's three coffee farms – was told that NORAD had notified Brazilian authorities about the UFOs.

In his book about the incident, *Incidente em Varginha*, Pacaccini said that in Belo Horizonte in July 1996, a Brazilian Air Force officer told him NORAD had notified CINDACTA, the Brazilian civilian-military air traffic control system, and CINDACTA alerted the ESA Army command in Três Corações. This was on January 13, but what time of day or night is not known.

Other than one incident to be related in a moment, there were no UFO sightings in the vicinity of Varginha on January 13 or January 20, but many were reported throughout the region as well as around the country before and after those dates and continuing through much of the year.

THE CRASH, JANUARY 13

On Friday January 12, 35-year-old Carlos da Souza drove across São Paulo, one of the largest cities in the world, and checked into a hotel in the northern suburb of Mairiporã. He was going to Três Corações, about 150 miles to the north, and wanted to get an early start the next morning.

Souza owned an exterminating business and his hobby is flying ultra light planes. He planned to meet other ultra light pilots in Três Corações to arrange for a competition.

He awakened at four o'clock on the morning of Saturday, January 13, got into his red pickup truck and headed north on the heavily traveled Fernão Dias Highway (BR 381) which connects São Paulo and Belo Horizonte.

The drive was uneventful until about eight o'clock, when he was about three miles south of the intersection with MG 26, of a state highway that leads to Varginha to the west and Três Corações to the east. A muffled roaring sound interrupted his thoughts, and he wondered if something was wrong with the truck.

He stopped to check but when he stepped down from the cab he realized the noise was coming from a cigar-shaped craft about 400 feet in the air just west of the highway. The sun was reflecting off it.

The craft was traveling north, almost parallel to the highway, at forty to fifty miles an hour. It was silver-colored and appeared to be thirty to forty feet long and twelve to fifteen wide.

It had at least four windows along the side and what looked like a big jagged hole four or five feet in diameter in the front. There was a long dent or crack running from the hole back to the middle of the craft, from which point white smoke or vapor was coming out.

Astonished and excited, Souza jumped in his pickup and followed the UFO for about ten miles. It soon crossed over to the east side of the highway and eventually passed over some small mountains. Then it went into a sharp thirty-degree dive and disappeared from sight.

Souza thought it had crashed and began looking for a way to get to the area. About twenty minutes later he found a dirt road and turned onto it.

Minutes later he drove over the crest of a hill and there before him was wreckage spread all over a hilly field of knee-high grass. He also saw about forty soldiers and two male nurses, two trucks, a helicopter, an ambulance and three cars. All were Army vehicles.

Everyone was busily running around picking up pieces of debris. One truck already held a chunk half the size of a mini-van. A strong smell of ammonia and ether hung in the air.

It was a terrible crash and Souza doubted that anyone had lived through it. He was surprised to see anyone there, let alone the military. He didn't know at the time that the site was only seven miles from the ESA Army base in Três Corações.

He parked and walked toward the wreckage, thinking he could help. He picked up a piece of aluminum-like material that was very light. It floated to the ground when he dropped it.

Then one of the men spotted him, shouted, and in an instant, armed soldiers rushed toward him. They ordered him to leave immediately. He protested, thinking someone had been badly hurt or killed, but a corporal screamed at him to get out and that "this is none of your business!"

Souza got back in his truck and drove away. But he was so astounded by what he'd seen that he abandoned his trip and headed back toward São Paulo. About ten minutes later, he stopped at a roadside restaurant to have coffee and think about what had happened.

The emotional impact was so great that he was still sitting there two hours later when a car drove up with two men. They were in civilian clothes but military haircuts and bearing. One got out and walked up to him, asked if his name was Carlos da Souza, then asked what he'd seen.

"I saw everything and I know something happened there," Souza said.

"You haven't seen anything," the man replied, then related many details of Souza's personal life. "You live on such and such a road, in such and such a city, you're married to so and so, and you're the father of so many children, and your mother is so and so. If you tell people what you saw, it's going to be very bad for you. We already have a complete printout on your whole life."

Such personal information is readily available to authorities by computer once someone's license number is known. The man warned Souza not to say anything to anybody, and then left.

All this occurred on January 13, one week before the three women saw the creature in nearby Varginha, but for nine months Souza told no one except his wife and two close friends.

He explained that he was frightened by the man's threat. A twenty-year military dictatorship had ended only a few years earlier, and some of Souza's relatives "disappeared" during the dictatorship, so he kept quiet.

He was not aware of the "ETs" in Varginha until the following September when he read a magazine article written by Claudeir Covo, a São Paulo safety engineer and a lifelong ufologist who had been working with Ubirajara and Pacaccini.

Souza contacted Covo, who eventually persuaded him to return to Varginha to show him and Ubirajara where he had seen the wreckage.

An inspection of the area – now nine months later – showed no indication that a crash had occurred, nor was Ubirajara subsequently able to find any farmers, farm workers or anyone else in the area who knew anything about a crash.

Not everyone believes Souza's story, and even Ubirajara and Covo (it was Covo who told us what Souza said) have reservations about it because no other witnesses could be found. Also, some elements of his story were similar to things that had been portrayed in the movie *Roswell*.

In addition, Souza's description of the UFO was almost identical to one seen by a farm couple on the morning of January 20 that the investigators – and much of the public – had known about since early in the investigation.

However, on a later visit to the site, Ubirajara and members of his Varginha UFO group found an area of ground about 400 feet square that seemed to have been replaced by sod.

Furthermore, during the early stages of the investigation, several military witnesses said they had seen pieces of a crashed craft being transported into ESA by two Army trucks on January 13, and that later the wreckage was convoyed to the national aerospace center in São José dos Campos near São Paulo.

"There are things that favored Souza's report," Ubirajara told us, "but we have to say we could not verify it."

THE FARM COUPLE, JANUARY 20

Early on the morning of Saturday, January 20, on a farm six miles east of Varginha, Oralina de Freitas, then 37, was awakened by the sound of cattle milling around, mooing and bellowing. A digital clock on the bedside table said one-fourteen in the morning.

Oralina opened the window and saw the cattle were very agitated and stampeding all over the pasture 300 to 400 feet away. Then she saw a cigar-shaped object just above the cattle. There was no moon but the craft gave off a faint light.

Oralina called out to her husband, Eurico, 40, and he rushed to the window. "My God!" he cried. "There's a submarine above my pasture."

They could see gray smoke or vapor coming out of the back as it moved slowly, in a sort of rocking motion, only fifteen to twenty feet above the ground.

Neither Eurico nor Oralina ventured outside, but stood at the window watching as the object took forty-five minutes to pass ever so slowly out of sight over a ridge about 2,000 feet away, heading in the direction of Varginha.

They had the impression that it was having difficulties of some kind because of the very slow way it was moving. If the UFO was making any sound, the bellowing of the cows drowned it out.

All this time, the cattle remained panicky and frightened, but the couple's four dogs, although awake, showed no reaction. Eurico and Oralina's four children, aged 12 to 20, slept through it all.

Ubirajara learned about the incident six days later. The couple, who oversee the farm, told the owner what happened. He in turn told a friend of Ubirajara's who passed the story on to him.

The farm house is only about five miles cross country from the spot where Carlos da Souza said he first saw a similar UFO on January 13.

THE MORNING CAPTURE, JANUARY 20

In Brazil, the Military Police are not members of a military organization or part of the armed forces. Instead, they are state police under the control of a state's governor.

Military policemen perform a variety of duties, including patrolling highways, putting down riots, and rescuing people in floods and other disasters. They are also the firemen for the entire nation, and one of their duties as firefighters is capturing mad dogs, wild animals, and dangerous snakes.

It was in this latter capacity that four firemen answered a call around eight-thirty on the morning of January 20 about a strange creature being seen near the woods in Jardim Andere. One or more persons had phoned police, who alerted the Fire Department.

By the time the firemen responded, three boys 12 to 14 years old had seen the creature as they were walking along Rua Suécia. This is the first street above the woods and runs parallel to the woods. A steep, 200-foot-long embankment begins at the street level and leads down to the railroad tracks and the woods just beyond.

As the kids were watching, a man and a woman came walking by, not together, and they saw the creature also. At this time the creature was slowly shuffling down the precipitous bank toward the woods. The boys had been throwing stones at it trying to get a reaction from it, but the woman told them to stop.

When the firemen arrived in a fire truck, they told everyone to leave immediately, saying it was a secret Army operation. By then the creature had disappeared into the woods.

Wearing their regular uniforms and heavy gloves and carrying nets, the firemen went down the bank, crossed the tracks and entered the woods in search of the creature.

It took them two hours to capture it, partly because it kept running away from them in the dense growth, and partly because they didn't know what it was and they were wary of it. They caught glimpses of it from time to time but it kept scurrying away from them.

If you walk into the woods, as we have, it's easy to see why the creature was able to elude the firemen for so long. Thick, tangled bushes and countless trees prevent you from seeing very far, and the footing is tricky even when following one of the paths. The terrain is rough and uneven, all up and down with almost no level areas. Cars and trucks can be heard on nearby streets but are seldom seen.

When the men were finally able to throw a net over the creature, it offered no resistance. It made a buzzing or humming sound as they struggled up the hill with it in the net.

At some time during the search, one of the firemen had returned to the truck and radioed his commander, told him what was happening and asked him to join them. By the time the creature was carried up to the street, the commander had arrived – as had an Army truck with two officers and a sergeant. It is believed that the fire commander had notified them.

The firemen handed the creature over to the Army men with little or no discussion. It was put in a wooden box, which was then covered by a canvas and put in the back of the truck with two men sitting beside it. The truck then left in a hurry to return to the Army base in Três Corações. The firemen and their commander then returned to the fire station.

The Jogger, January 20

Some time between one-thirty and two in the afternoon, a jogger saw seven armed soldiers cross a small footbridge from Santana and enter the pasture next to the woods in Jardim Andere. The pasture is on the side of a long hill leading five to six hundred yards up to the railroad tracks and Suécia Street above, where the fire truck had parked that morning.

Two of the soldiers were carrying automatic rifles and all were wearing side arms. Two also carried small rectangular, aluminum-colored boxes or suitcases.

The jogger wondered what they were doing. He had intended to take a short cut down through the pasture and across the same bridge but changed his mind.

The soldiers grouped into a *V* formation and moved up the hill. They searched a small grove of trees just below the tracks, apparently found nothing, then turned and moved toward the big woods.

The jogger, seeing them enter the woods, continued straight ahead for several blocks and then turned to his right into the street that leads through the woods to Santana. Just a minute or so later, he heard three distinct shots.

Astonished and extremely curious, the jogger returned to the street that overlooks the woods and saw an army truck with soldiers in it now parked there.

At that moment, four of the soldiers who had gone into the woods came struggling up the steep embankment carrying two bags, two soldiers to each bag. One bag was squirming as if something alive was in it, but the other had no movement.

The bags were heaved into the truck, the soldiers climbed in and the truck sped away.

Just what was in the bags is not known. However, it would seem safe to assume it wouldn't take seven armed soldiers to capture a wild animal when four firemen without weapons had captured another "wild animal" in the same woods a few hours earlier and had turned it over to Army personnel without any discussion.

CREATURE ENCOUNTER, JANUARY 20

This was the encounter the three women had. For some weeks the only thing most people knew about the "Varginha ET" was that Liliane, Valquíria and Kátia had seen a creature at three o'clock in the afternoon on January 20.

That incident, described in detail earlier, was publicized literally around the world. But, as we now know, it was just one in a series of related events.

THE STORM, JANUARY 20

Luiza da Silva, the mother of the two sisters, said that when she and Kátia went to the vacant lot, they saw an impression in the grass where the creature had been and they also noticed a strong odor. But less than three hours later all that vanished.

"There was a hailstorm at six o'clock that was absolutely unprecedented," said Ubirajara. "It lasted only three or four minutes but it broke windshields and everything and wiped out all traces of the creature in the vacant lot."

THE DEATH OF AN OFFICER

During or just after the storm, soldiers and military policemen continued their search. Among them were two plainclothes Military

Police agents who spotted yet another creature – possibly the one that the three women had seen that afternoon. It was hiding in a construction site in the Santana-Jardim Andere area not far from the woods.

The two men were able to capture it and force it into the back seat of their unmarked police car. It may have been ill because the men reportedly took it to a small public health clinic for treatment. However, the doctor there refused to go near the creature and told them to take it to a hospital.

Sometime during all this, one of the officers, 23-year-old Marco Chereze, stopped by his parents' house, soaked from the rain. He told his mother he was on a mission and would be working all night. He asked her to tell his wife he wouldn't be home for dinner, changed his clothes and left.

Only Chereze is believed to have handled the creature with his bare hands while capturing it, and he became gravely ill some days later with an unusual infection. He was admitted to a hospital with a very high fever.

He rapidly lost use of his arms and legs, and was unable to feed himself. At the end, he turned blue and failed to respond to treatment. He died on February 15.

The only advice authorities gave his family was that his coffin should be sealed, that the funeral should take place without delay, and that burial should take place within a few hours.

His father later recalled that several weeks earlier when rumors of ETs first began to circulate, Marco was convinced that this was only the beginning of a lot of trouble.

Marco's grandmother said that one night when the first reports of ETs came out in the newspapers, she was watching TV with him and his wife when a movie about aliens came on. Marco immediately switched the set off and said sharply: "Don't watch that – it's nonsense!" His outburst was puzzling and he offered no explanation.

Chereze's family reportedly sued the Military Police because:

1. The cause of his death was never explained;
2. The results of any autopsy were never revealed – the only thing of note was a lab report saying a "small quantity of toxic material" had been found in his body – and;
3. Allegedly his official records were altered to state that he wasn't on duty that night.

THE CREATURE AT THE ZOO, APRIL 21

On the evening of April 21, Terezinha Clepf, her husband, and some friends attended a birthday party at a restaurant in Varginha's zoo. Around nine o'clock, after Mrs. Clepf finished eating, she went outside to sit on the verandah by herself and smoke a cigarette. After several minutes, she began to feel uneasy.

"I felt that someone was looking at me," she said later. The porch was dark but some light was coming from the restaurant. "I turned to my left and saw a strange creature staring at me."

It was about fifteen feet away and appeared to be four to five feet tall. "I didn't know what it was, an animal or whatever," Mrs. Clepf, then 67, said.

"It was very ugly. It was brown and had a brightness or shininess to the skin. The eyes were big and red and the mouth was just a stroke. He stayed there looking at me."

She was so terrified she could barely move for several minutes. Then, afraid to make any sudden movement, she slowly got up and walked back inside. She looked back once and the creature was still staring at her. It was several days before she could tell her husband about it.

THE ZOO DEATHS

After that incident was publicized, Leila Cabral, director of the zoo, contacted Ubirajara and Pacaccini and told them that five animals had mysteriously died at the zoo about a week before Mrs. Clepf's experience. An anteater, two deer, a blue macaw, and a bobcat died suddenly and unexpectedly.

The anteater was healthy and tame. It died because of an "unidentified toxic substance," Ms. Cabral said. The deer died of "caustic intoxication without apparent cause" and no cause of death could be determined for the macaw and bobcat.

THE THREAT TO THE SISTERS

Around ten o'clock on the night of May 3 or 4, Liliane and Valquíria da Silva and their mother Luiza were asleep at their home in Santana when someone knocked on the front door. The father was working as a fare collector on a bus and the family's two older daughters were at school.

Mrs. Silva went to the front door and saw four men dressed in dark suits. She thought they were associated with Ubirajara but soon realized they were strangers. By then, however, the men had gently pushed their way inside and insisted on talking to Liliane and Valquíria.

Luiza got the girls up and everyone gathered in the small living room, with the girls and mother sitting on one sofa, the four men on another sofa opposite them.

One man was about 50, the others in their early 30s. They were polite but businesslike. Only the older man and one of the others talked.

They never identified themselves but spent more than an hour trying to get the girls to change their story and even implied they would be paid a lot of money if they made their denials publicly on TV.

Afraid to object, Luiza said they would think it over.

"They never raised their voices but we felt intimidated," Liliane told us when we talked to her for the second time in 1997.

The men finally left but told them not to follow them or try to see what kind of car they were driving. The men were never seen again and the girls did not withdraw their story.

HIGHWAY SIGHTING, MAY 15

A 21-year-old biology student, Ildo Lúcio Gordino, was driving from Três Corações to Varginha around seven-thirty that night. As he was rounding a curve, a strange animal started to cross the highway.

"I had slowed because of the curve," Ildo said. "About forty meters ahead the headlights shone on a dark brown thing with hair all over its body. It had huge eyes that reflected red in the headlights. It covered its face with its hands and crouched down."

Ildo was badly frightened and he drove past the creature, which rose up and hurried back into the bushes.

When Ubirajara and Pacaccini investigated, they were surprised to find it had happened almost in front of the farm where Eurico and Oralina de Freitas had seen a UFO on January 20.

THE PASSOS CREATURE

A seventh creature was seen several times in May 1996 in Passos, a city about forty miles north of Varginha, but whether it should be included as part of the "Varginha ET" case is questionable because this one was violent.

A 20-year-old man named Luciano said he was walking home late one dark night when a hairy creature about five-foot-five and with a strange growl jumped out from the trees and attacked him. Luciano is six-foot-five and weighed a hundred and ninety pounds but was knocked to the ground, his shirt and jacket ripped by sharp claws.

He kicked out and knocked the creature off balance, jumped up and ran but was knocked down again. In the scuffle, Luciano kicked the creature in the groin, causing it to double over, and Luciano was finally able to escape to a nearby house.

Pacaccini investigated the incident and he saw Luciano's injuries and torn clothing. He is convinced Luciano was telling the truth.

A week later Pacaccini and another investigator found three other persons in Passos who said they too had been attacked. Not knowing what the creature was and for lack of a more accurate term, all four victims described it as a "werewolf. "

Pacaccini believes the Passos creature is real and unexplained but doubts it is related to the Varginha creatures because of its size, hairiness and vicious nature.

"We are talking about a completely different creature, in a totally different situation," Pacaccini said.

THE AMERICANS

Almost from the beginning, some investigators were convinced that the creatures, dead and alive, had been taken to the United States. This conviction was based largely on:

1. The belief that these creatures truly were from some place other than Earth, and
2. Statements made by disgruntled military personnel who resented the idea that Brazil would relinquish control of the aliens and turn them over to the U.S.

This conviction was further strengthened in early March 1996 – just five weeks after the initial incidents – by the visit to São Paulo and other parts of Brazil of Warren Christopher, then U.S. Secretary of State, and NASA Director Daniel S. Goldin, ostensibly to arrange for a Brazilian astronaut to join a future Space Shuttle flight.

CONCLUSIONS:

We have felt from the very beginning that this is a strong case. There were just too many witnesses, even though most of them cannot be identified for fear of official retribution.

It was probably inevitable that, from the beginning, the case would be compared to Roswell. The constant denials by authorities indicate an official cover-up – as many believe is true in the Roswell case. However, many ufologists now believe the Roswell case has been discredited.

The Varginha case, on the other hand, is still relatively fresh and UFO investigators were immediately able to gather considerable evidence, including testimony from more than two dozen firsthand witnesses.

The investigation continues, although it is doubtful that any of those witnesses will ever be able to come forward and tell publicly what they know, or whether the government will ever acknowledge what happened.

NOTE: All of the military and police personnel involved in this incident were reassigned to other parts of the country within months of the incident. The two chief investigators, Ubirajara Rodrigues and Vitório Pacaccini, have continued their investigations, but separately.

Each has also written a book about the case, both in Portuguese. Pacaccini published Incidente em Varginha in late 1996. Ubirajara's book, O Caso Varginha, was published in late 2001. Pacaccini has also written an English version that has not yet been published. (In March 2002, Pacaccini cut back on some of his business activities to enroll in a two-year university program that led to his earning a doctorate in business administration in 2004.)

Corrections Officers

Galway, New York

October 28, 1998

At 11 a.m., while driving to visit his mother, a New York State Corrections Officer (witness requested anonymity), his 11-year-old daughter, and her 10-year-old girl friend watched a light hovering in the sky. It moved as if to go higher in the sky, and then appeared to turn. As it turned, the light faded and revealed the crescent shape of a solid object. From a standstill position, it moved away in a steady straight line until it flew out of sight. The entire sighting lasted about only one minute. A few minutes later, an Air Force jet was seen flying in the same direction, though the witness believed this was unrelated.[58]

UFO Incident at Lackland Air Force Base in Texas

During the summer of 1999, Frank Soriano was working at the Washington Correctional Facility in upstate New York. One day, while waiting for roll call, a group of correctional officers gathered outside at a picnic table adjacent to the Administration Building to chat about nothing in particular. Frank sat out there listening and joking with the others.

One of Frank's friends, Matt R., brought up the subject of UFOs and then mentioned Frank's video of the UFO seen over Ticonderoga, New York, on July 2, 1998. Another officer made a disbelieving remark, and a third officer, Ross M. (Frank's partner in the Special Housing Unit) stepped forward and stated that it was true that Frank had a video of a UFO. At this, conversation stopped and everyone listened intently. Ross is a very imposing figure, at six-foot-three, highly intelligent, and while working in the Air Force on missiles, he had special clearance.

Frank told all of the officers that what he had captured on film was as real as the cars parked out in the facility parking lot, and was not fiction or his imagination but a flying craft that had no wings and was big and silent.

Another, very well-respected officer interjected. "Frank's right. UFOs are real. I know this because I saw one first hand." The speaker, Officer George P. from Vermont, was the oldest officer in the group and one of the most respected. For the first time in all the years we've known him, he had stepped forward to admit something that most people would take to their graves. A hush fell over the group as we listened closely to his every word.

George told everyone that he had at one time been an Air Traffic Controller in the eighties until President Reagan put an end to that career when he fired most of the air traffic controllers for going on strike. And long before that, he was an air traffic controller while in the Air Force and stationed at Lackland Air Force base in Texas, when an incident took place on December 24, 1964 that completely changed his way of looking at life.

That night, he was working the tower with a Gunney Sergeant and it was just past 7 p.m. on Christmas Eve. Because of the holiday, the base was nearly deserted, only George and the Sarge present.   George said he had lit up a cigarette and was just staring out at the large field. After about a minute, he noticed color lights in the air descending toward the airfield. The lights were so far apart from each other that at first he thought that they appeared to be independent objects. But as the lights got closer to the ground, he realized that all of the lights were attached to one huge object. He said that it was massive. It was circular and it was domed with a diameter of over 3,800 feet and dark, dull gray in color. When questioned by one of the officers as to how he was so sure that it was over 3,800 feet in diameter, George quickly replied because it overlapped all four runways that are parallel to each other and the distance across all four runways is 3,800 feet.

He stated that he and the Gunney Sarge were frozen at the tower window staring at this thing. The craft hovered at about 100 feet above the runway and at a distance of about 700 to 800 feet from the tower.

George said he had picked up the phone and attempted to call the base commander to report the UFO, when the Sarge yanked it out of his hand and shouted, "What are you doing?"

George told him that he was going to call the base commander.

The Sarge yelled back, "No you're not!"

When George asked why not, the Sarge told him that the last time he had reported a UFO to the military was about seven years ago. He had then been locked up and away from his family for six months. He was still being debriefed on that incident, and he had never been able to rise in rank since that time. He said that he was never going to go through that again.

George said that the Sarge just stood by the phone, fear and anger in his eyes, and George knew that he meant business. During this time, the craft just hovered over the field and stayed there for over five hours. It did not register on the radar scope.

Approximately fifteen or twenty minutes after the craft first arrived, four small UFOs emerged from underneath the large craft minutes apart from each other. They each lowered from the center of the large craft and moved straight, silent, and slowly until they reached the rim of the larger craft and then shot off at a tremendous speed into the dark. Each of the small UFOs were identical and appeared to be operated the same as the others.

Shortly after midnight, all four of the small UFOs returned, coming in at a tremendous speed until they reached the rim of the larger craft. They moved to the center of the craft, then appeared to rise up into it. Moments later, the large craft rose up, with lights blinking different colors – red, blue, green, amber, and white. As it rose, there was no sound and no exhaust. It slowly gained momentum and then shot up into the night sky.

Frank asked George if he thought that the craft might have belonged to our government. George replied, "AB-SO-LUTE-LY NOT." He added that he and the Sarge never discussed that incident ever again.[59]

As a side note to this report, in his book, *UFOs and the National Security State* by Richard Dolan, five years to the date prior to this sighting, the Inspector General of the Air Force issued the following warning regarding UFOs to every air base commander in the continental United States.

> Unidentified flying objects—sometimes treated lightly by the press and referred to as "Flying Saucers" must be rapidly and accurately identified as serious US Air Force business in Z1 (interior zone).... Technical and defense considerations will continue to exist in this area.

It is also noted that UFO investigators sent out from air bases:

> ...should be equipped with binoculars, camera, Geiger counter, magnifying glass and source for containers in which to store samples.[60]

STONY CREEK, NY

A retired NYS Corrections Officer recalled an incident that happened in his childhood during the early 1970s. He told of watching a UFO from inside his home in Stony Creek, New York with his brother and sisters. Les stepped outside of the house and left his siblings inside so he could get a better look at the object. He described the object as being about 100 feet in diameter, domed, and colored dark gray. The object was hovering only about four feet off the ground in a nearby field. He was about halfway to the object from the house as his brother and sisters kept crying for him to return to the house. His last recollection of the incident was looking back to the house and then to the object. Neither he nor his siblings can remember anything beyond that point in time.

THE GOVERNMENT
AND UFO INVOLVEMENT

As hard as the government appears to stay out of the UFO phenomena, it is buried deep in conspiracy, from the alleged UFO crash in Roswell, New Mexico, in 1947, to the current sightings. Whether it is an individual politician or a large military, or other governmental agency, suspicions of hiding information about UFOs mar the integrity of our government in the eyes of the millions of UFO witnesses who want to know the truth, and to feel free to speak about it publicly without fear of retribution or ridicule.

The government hasn't tried to stay out of the controversy. It has even tried to get involved and on occasion, and has investigated the situation in a credible manner. But many suspect that they found out a few things that they didn't want to reveal, and went into the business of debunking sightings and ridiculing witnesses even to the point of harassment. Laws have been enacted to silence military witnesses, and some people have even accused military organizations of threatening their lives in order to prevent them from talking about what they've seen.

For a subject that the government says has no merit to it and not worthy of investigating, a lot of time and effort has been put into determining how to deal with the public and how to explain away things that have been seen and documented by some very credible witnesses.

Stonewalling by agencies such as the CIA, NSA, FBI, NASA, Air Force, just to name a few, is a tactic that has been used to prevent UFO organizations, witnesses, celebrities, and even other politicians such as Presidents, senators, and governors from getting information about the subject.

The FOIA (Freedom of Information Act), which was enacted in 1966, has been used to obtain documents dealing with government UFO dealings. People such as Stanton Friedman and John Greenewald (www. blackvault.com) have used the FOIA to obtain such documents, only to come up with reams of pages that are blank or that have so many lines blacked out that they are practically unreadable. If there is nothing to this subject and no threat to our country, why is so much text blacked out? The government claims that there is vital information on the pages that involves national security.

What national security issues could be on a page that pertains to a subject that doesn't exist and is no threat to us? And why are there so many documents on the subject, if it isn't important enough to investigate any more?

The truth about our government and UFOs will one day come out, because you can never hold back the inevitable. Time will see to that.

THE GOVERNMENT GETS INVOLVED
IN THEIR OWN INVESTIGATIONS
ROBERTSON PANEL

January 14 – 18, 1953
The last week of the Truman Presidency

In 1953, a secret committee was formed to debunk UFOs and to steer the incoming Eisenhower administration away from giving UFO research a serious consideration, at least publicly.

On January 14, a small group of scientists, governmental officials and Air Force representatives met over a four-day period. They discussed the interests that the CIA and the OSI had on the subject of UFOs and then they were updated regarding the activities of Project Blue Book. The next day, General W. M. Garland, Chief of Air Technical Intelligence Center, attended the meeting and gave the group three objectives.

1. He wanted to increase the use of thoroughly briefed Air Force Intelligence Officers to investigate UFOs.
2. He wanted to have as many UFO reports declassified as possible.
3. He wanted to increase the size of Project Blue Book.

At the conclusion of the four-day meeting, the panel came up with an aim at debunking the numerous UFO sightings being reported. They also decided that certain civilian UFO groups needed to be watched. They decided to set up an "educational" means to get the public to think that not all UFO sightings needed to be investigated and to use the media in their debunking scheme. [61]

CONDON REPORT

University of Colorado in 1965

Due to public outcry of cover ups of the UFO situation, a call from then-Senator Gerald Ford to study the effectiveness of the UFO investigations by the government, and the Air Force's wishes to put an end to rumors of a cover up, the Air Force approached several universities to study the UFO investigations that had been conducted. The University of Colorado agreed to take on the project, and a physical scientist named Edward Condon was appointed to lead the study. The committee was composed of scientists who were nearly all skeptical of UFOs.

This study began in October of 1966, and at the end, the committee determined that all but about thirty percent of the cases they reviewed could be explained by mundane objects or events. It is astonishing that with so many cases still unidentified, many took the results as proof that there is no reality to the UFO issue.

A problem that the committee had tried to avoid was being labeled not too fair and pre-judging the study even before it began. This was not helped by the behavior of Dr. Condon, who was quoted in the upstate New York newspaper, the *Elmira Star-Gazette*, in January, 1967 as saying:

> It is my inclination right now to recommend that the government get out of this business. My attitude right now is that there is nothing to it.

"With a smile," the newspaper said, Condon added:

> But, I'm not supposed to reach a conclusion for another year.

While the committee was still conducting their study, and before they were to present their conclusion, the *New York Times* ran this headline in the January 8, 1968 issue:

UFO, Findings:
No Visits From Afar

> The author stated that the Colorado Project would debunk the ETH (Extra-terrestrial Hypothesis Explanation) and dismiss the demands for a large scale effort to determine the nature of "flying saucers."[62]

NASA

NASA has pretty much tried to stay out of the limelight of the UFO controversy. The Air Force's few attempts to dump the subject into their lap had been unsuccessful. Yet there have been many reports of UFO sightings by people associated with NASA. Several astronauts have gone public with their beliefs and their sightings, which have occurred both here on Earth and in space. For a while, people were able to videotape off television some objects seen in space from NASA downlinks. NASA attempted to explain away many of the reports, and eventually instituted a delay on their broadcasts – many believe, in order to give them time to edit the images before releasing them to the public.

On October 17, 1993, as the Space Shuttle *Columbia STS -58* was entering orbit at 222,000 feet. NASA film footage caught an object moving past and above the shuttle at a very high speed. The film footage of the UFO was freeze-framed and enlarged, showing what looked like two oval objects moving past the shuttle as one unit, with what appears to be a dark line vertically down the center of it. (This object is similar to the object that was both seen and videotaped crossing the sky over Ticonderoga, New York on July 2, 1998, and referred to as the "Flying Peanut" – more on this later.)[63]

A similar report, although not from NASA, states that, during the mid-1970s, a young Russian Cosmonaut named Vladmir Kovalyonok witnessed a UFO while orbiting the Earth in the Russian craft Soyuz. He observed what appeared to be two oval objects with a line down the center of it, moving in unison as one structure. He then watched them separate into two UFOs and move in different directions. This cosmonaut is now a Lt. General. In his drawing, the object he saw appears to be identical to the UFO seen over Ticonderoga, New York in 1998.[64]

Many of the NASA Astronauts have had UFO experiences in space as well as on Earth. Some have come forward with what they have seen and some still choose to keep quiet about it. Here are some of the comments by those willing to admit their sightings:

FRANK BORMAN

In December of 1965, during the second orbit of his record-breaking flight with James Lovell, Borman reported seeing an unidentified flying object from his capsule *Gemini 7*. When reporting the object to Gemini Control, he was told that he was looking at the final stage of their own booster rocket. Borman said he could see the booster rocket, but he was also looking at something that was not from his rocket.[65]

JAMES LOVELL

To confirm Borman's report, James Lovell notified Gemini Control at Cape Kennedy that he also saw many other objects while the rocket stage booster was visible.[66]

GORDON COOPER

Cooper reported that, in 1951, while piloting an F-86 Saber Jet over Western Germany, he saw some saucer-shaped metallic discs at considerable altitude. These objects were able to out maneuver all of American fighter jets.

Major Cooper also testified many years later before the United Nations that he believed that the extraterrestrial vehicles and their crews are visiting this planet from other planets.[67]

NEIL ARMSTRONG, EUGENE CERNAN, AND BUZZ ALDRIN

On his historic first landing on the moon along with astronauts Eugene Cernan and Buzz Aldrin, Neil Armstrong reported seeing objects on the moon that were not from Earth. When asked to describe what he was seeing, Armstrong said, "These babies are huge sir! Enormous, oh my God, you wouldn't believe it." He said also, "There are other space craft out there, lined up on the far side of the crater's edge. They are on the moon watching us."[68]

JOSEPH A. WALKER

During his record breaking fifty-mile-high flight in April, 1962, NASA test pilot Joseph Walker reported filming UFOs for the second time while in flight. In a lecture some years later, he refused to speculate about UFOs. He stated, "All I know is what appeared on the film which was developed after the flight." None of the films have ever been released to the public.[69]

ROBERT WHITE

During his July, 1962, fifty-eight-mile-high flight, of an X-15, Major White reported seeing a UFO. He stated, "I have no idea what it could be. It was grayish in color and about 30 to 40 feet away." *Time Magazine* had quoted him as saying in a broadcast back to base, "There ARE things out there! There absolutely is!"[70]

THE PROJECTS

Since 1947, the Army-Air Force was bombarded with reports of sightings of flying saucers. The military publicly admitted that it had captured a "Flying Saucer" one day, and then changed their story to that of mistaken identification of a weather balloon. Witnesses were calling into radio stations, newspaper, police stations, and the government, and all turned to the Army-Air Force to answer their questions. Were there flying saucers or not? Were we being visited by extraterrestrials, or was there a natural explanation?

What was the military to do? At that point, no one really knew what was happening.

Or did they?

They started an investigative project known as Project Sign, but soon realized that this was not helping their situation. Reports were still coming in and there was no official explanation from the government. Project Sign had to go and the Air Force decided that they needed to tone down the interest in UFOs. So they created Project Grudge. This time the government's tone changed from one of curiosity and learning to that of harassment and ridicule. This didn't work either because too many complaints from the public forced the Air Force to try and compromise a little. Eventually, Project Blue Book became the official Air Force investigative unit to ease the public's concerns about what is out there and how the military could deal with it. In 1969, the Air Force announced that they had determined that UFOs were not a threat to national security and no longer worth the resources being spent on it, and Project Blue Book was terminated. The Air Force was no longer involved in UFO investigations, at least publicly.

PROJECT SIGN

In January 1948, the Air Force officially got into the business of UFO investigations. Named Project Sign, it was also known by its nickname, Project Saucer. Headquartered by Air Material Command out of Wright Field, which became known as Wright Patterson Air Force base, its function was to openly and fair-mindedly investigate UFOs and to determine whether these objects posed a threat to the United States, and whether they might be of extraterrestrial origin.

By fall, the group had come up with their "Estimate of the Situation" in which they expressed the opinion that at least some UFOs were of extraterrestrial origin. This did not sit well with those in command at the Air Force, so the estimate was rejected and ordered to be destroyed. The Air Force later claimed that no such Estimate report ever existed.[71]

PROJECT GRUDGE

In December 1948, Project Sign was terminated, but investigation into UFOs continued under Project Grudge, beginning in February 1949. As its name implies, this group had an agenda from the beginning – to diminish public interest in UFOs by identifying them as mundane objects. There was no serious consideration that UFOs were extraterrestrial, but they had to be identified as either man-made objects, hoaxes, or mistaken identifications of natural weather phenomena. The goal of Project Grudge was not to solve the UFO phenomena, but to explain it away. The mind set was now that UFOs do not exist.

One of the efforts of the new group was to use the media to downplay the UFO situation. One article printed in the *Saturday Evening Post* explained UFO sightings as mistakes, hoaxes, or gullibility. The Air Force was convinced that this strategy would work, and it might have, but for the writer's brief mention that some sightings still hadn't been explained. Soon after the article, a new rash of sightings were reported. All attempts by the Air Force to explain away the reports only seemed to convince the public that they were seeing things that cannot be explained away. Soon Project Grudge lost its effectiveness and had to be shut down in December of 1949. However, the UFO question would not go away.[72]

PROJECT BLUE BOOK

Project Blue Book was created by the Air Force after the previous UFO investigative projects failed at what they had hoped to do, which was to explain away the interest in UFOs and discourage people from reporting them. However, it had to be done more carefully than before, as Project Grudge had shown that the public was not so easily fooled by dogmatic statements that ignored facts.

With Project Blue Book, the Air Force had three main objectives:

1. First, to try to find an explanation for all reports of UFO sightings;
2. Second, to determine whether these objects posed any threat to the security of the United States; and

3. Third, to determine whether any advanced UFO technology could be used by the United States.

Despite their early ideals, Project Blue Book became a public relations program. Sightings were identified even in cases where no reasonable explanation could be given, by ignoring evidence and witness accounts. Witnesses were labeled crackpots without any investigation into their credibility, and their stories discounted. In some cases, explanations were given to cases that were years old and classified as unidentified at the time. As a result of the findings of the Condon Committee through the University of Colorado, the Air Force finally decided to shut down Project Blue Book.

When Project Blue Book was closed, the Air Force had determined that UFOs posed no threat to the United States, that there was no indication that UFOs represented any advanced technology beyond what we had already, and that there was no evidence that UFOs were extraterrestrial vehicles.[73]

UFO Sightings by Politicians & Celebrities

The following individuals, although not law enforcement officers, are credible respectable citizens who have had UFO experiences.

Although UFO sightings have been recorded almost as far back as history itself, many consider 1947 to be the beginning start of the modern day UFO era. This was the year of Kenneth Arnold's famous UFO sighting from his small plane, and the year of the alleged UFO crash in Roswell, New Mexico. Since then, a number of high-ranking government officials have dealt with the subject in one way or another. Most of them are merely witnesses, but some have had a little more to do with the decision making in how to handle the situation. Later, we will discuss an alleged government organization that may have taken over full control of what to do and how to do it. For now, we will consider the involvement of the United State's Presidents since 1947.

Several of our Presidents, including Richard Nixon, Jimmy Carter, and Ronald Reagan have gone on the record as having witnessed the UFO phenomenon. These men have been brave enough to admit publicly that they saw something in the sky that they could not identify.

President Roosevelt

There seems to be only a little information about any dealings that President Franklin D. Roosevelt had with UFO sightings. The primary dealing that may or may not have been associated with UFOs during Roosevelt's term was an alert that the city of Los Angeles was being attacked by UFOs.

On February 25, 1942, at 2:25 a.m., air raid sirens were heard throughout Los Angeles and the power was turned off to the area. It may just have been, as speculated, a lot of panic due to the relatively short time after the bombings of Pearl Harbor. When everything was done and the alert was lifted, it was discovered that there were six people dead. Three were killed by mortar shelling and three died of heart attacks during the commotion.

No enemy planes were identified and no country claimed credit for an invasion. Witnesses have said that during the attack all they could see was a huge object hovering over the city during the entire time that it was being fired upon by the military. The object was not damaged and when the shooting ended, it just moved slowly until it was out of sight.

To try and explain what had happened, General George C. Marshall wrote a memo to President Roosevelt. (See memo on page: Dinah add page number at layout)

WAR DEPARTMENT
OFFICE OF THE CHIEF OF STAFF
WASHINGTON

February 26, 1942.

MEMORANDUM FOR THE PRESIDENT:

The following is the information we have from GHQ at this moment regarding the air alarm over Los Angeles of yesterday morning:

"From details available at this hour:

"1. Unidentified airplanes, other than American Army or Navy planes, were probably over Los Angeles, and were fired on by elements of the 37th CA Brigade (AA) between 3:12 and 4:15 AM. These units expended 1430 rounds of ammunition.

"2. As many as fifteen airplanes may have been involved, flying at various speeds from what is officially reported as being 'very slow' to as much as 200 MPH and at elevations from 9000 to 18000 feet.

"3. No bombs were dropped.

"4. No casualties among our troops.

"5. No planes were shot down.

"6. No American Army or Navy planes were in action.

"Investigation continuing. It seems reasonable to conclude that if unidentified airplanes were involved they may have been from commercial sources, operated by enemy agents for purposes of spreading alarm, disclosing location of antiaircraft positions, and slowing production through blackout. Such conclusion is supported by varying speed of operation and the fact that no bombs were dropped."

Chief of Staff.

Franklin D. Roosevelt Library
DECLASSIFIED
OD DIR. 5200.9 (9/27/58)
Date- 3-10-59
Signature- Carl L. Spicer

February 26, 1942

Dear Harry:

Who is responsible for the air alarm system in the United States? Can anyone other than an authorized official of the United States Army order an air alarm?

It seems to me that all comment in reference to air alarms should be made exclusively by the appropriate officials of the Department responsible.

I am writing this note in the light of the two alarms last night.

Very sincerely yours,

FRANKLIN D. ROOSEVELT

The Honorable
The Secretary of War.

FDR/lab

Not satisfied with the explanation from General Marshall, President Roosevelt sent out another memo to Secretary of State Harry Stimson. (See memo on page: Dinah add page number at layout)

Although President Roosevelt had died before the 1950s, and was not around for the following, the former First Lady Eleanor Roosevelt had her little part of UFO history. She was a hostess on a radio show for NBC called *NBC Today with Mrs. Roosevelt* during the early years of the 1950s. During her show, she expressed a great deal of interest in the phenomena of Unidentified Flying Objects. She would call some UFO witnesses up and interview them on the show.[74]

President Truman

The so-called modern-day era of ufology began during President Truman's term in office. Up until 1947, objects in the sky were mentioned in hush and not much publicity or credence was given to the topic. In 1947, the subject broke open when Kenneth Arnold experienced his famous sighting of objects in the air near Mt. Ranier, and described them to the media. Shortly afterward, an object believed to be an extraterrestrial craft crashed at Roswell, New Mexico, and the U.S. Army-Air Force told the world that they had captured a "Flying Saucer." World War II had recently ended and the Cold War was beginning. Any flying saucers seen were considered to be either from outer space or from a hostile country, most likely the Soviet Union or Germany.[75]

President Eisenhower

When President Eisenhower was in office, he is reported to have received a letter from President Truman in regard to the UFO crash in Roswell, New Mexico, and the formation of an alleged group known as the Majestic Twelve, an "above top secret" unit of scientists, political big shots, and military personnel assigned to deal with the UFO situation.[76]

President Nixon

President Richard Nixon was, according to comedian Jackie Gleason, a man who was very interested in UFOs. Nixon was said to have had a large collection of books on the subject.

For more about President Nixon and Jackie Gleason, see the comments about Jackie Gleason further on in this chapter.[77]

President Ford

During the 1960s, the government was at odds with UFO enthusiasts over the disclosure of what was known and what was being held back from the public.

At that time, Gerald Ford was a Congressman from the State of Michigan. As the House Minority Leader, he took steps to resolve the problem between the government and the public over the UFO controversy. With the backing of other congressmen, he insisted that Congress conduct an investigation into the matter.

A few days before the end of March 1965, Congressman Ford wrote a letter to the Armed Services Committee Chairman expressing his displeasure in the government's actions toward the subject.

> I think there may be substance in some of these reports and because I believe the American people are entitled to a more thorough explanation than has been given them by the Air Force to date… I think we owe it to the people to establish the credibility regarding UFOs and to produce the greatest possible enlightenment on this subject.

On April 5, 1965, Congress held a closed door hearing on the subject of UFOs. Only three people were invited to testify and none of them believed in UFOs. Only, Dr. J. Allen Hynek, a member of Project Blue Book, urged the scientific community to get involved in the study of UFOs and suggested that a civilian panel of scientists should do this.[78]

During his time in office as President, Ford never publicly took up the subject of UFOs again.

PRESIDENT CARTER

While he was Governor of Alabama, Jimmy Carter saw an object in the sky and reported it to NICAP, the National Investigative Committee on Aerial Phenomena. During his campaign for President, he promised that he would end the government secrecy to the UFO enigma. It was a promise that, unfortunately, he never kept. Even today, he admits that he saw something in the sky that day, but he still doesn't know what it was. It was just an unknown object; and now he says he doesn't believe that it was extraterrestrial.

> It was the damnedest thing I've ever seen. It was big, it was very bright, it changed colors, and it was about the size of the moon. We watched it for ten minutes, but none of us could figure out what it was. One thing's for sure, I'll never make fun of people who say they've seen unidentified objects in the sky. [79]

PRESIDENT REAGAN

President Reagan spoke to Steven Spielberg after a private screening of Spielberg's film, *ET: The Extraterrestrial*. The President leaned over, clapped Spielberg on the shoulder, and quietly commented, "You know, there aren't six people in this room who know how true this really is." Unfortunately, the sudden press of people approaching Spielberg and the President prevented Spielberg from pursuing the strange comment made by Reagan.

President Reagan also saw UFOs on at least two occasions, once on his ranch in California and once while flying in a small plane. In 1974, Reagan, then Governor of California, stated:

> I was in a plane last week when I looked out the window and saw this white light. It was zigzagging around. I went up to the pilot and said, "Have you ever seen anything like that?" He was shocked and he said, "Nope." And I said to him: "Let's follow it!" We followed it for several minutes. It was a bright white light. We followed it to Bakersfield, and all of a sudden to our utter amazement it went straight up into the heavens.

President Reagan showed his perception of UFOs at the United Nations General Assembly, September 21st, 1987, when he stated:

> In our obsession with antagonisms of the moment, we often forget how much unites all the members of humanity. Perhaps we need some outside, universal threat to make us recognize this common bond. I occasionally think how quickly our differences worldwide would vanish if we were facing an alien threat from outside this world. And yet, I ask you, is not an alien threat already among us? What could be more alien to universal aspirations of our peoples than war and the threat of war?
>
> I couldn't help but – when you stop to think that we're all God's children, wherever we live in the world – I couldn't help but say to him [Gorbachev] just how easy his task and mine might be if suddenly there was a threat to this world from some other species from another planet outside in the universe. We'd forget all the little local differences that we have between our countries and we would find out once and for all that we really are all human beings here on this Earth together. Well, I guess we can wait for some alien race to come down and threaten us, but I think that between us, we can bring about that realization.[80]

President George H. W. Bush

President Bush may or may not have been a witness to UFOs, but before he served as president, he was the head of the CIA, and was privy to all of the information that was available concerning the investigation and research of the UFO enigma.

Senator Barry Goldwater

Senator Barry Goldwater had long had an interest in UFOs, and made several attempts to learn whether there was a recovered UFO at Wright Patterson Air Force Base. According to Richard Dolan's book *UFOs and the National Security State*, in 1957 he said:

> I frankly feel there is a great deal to this.

In *The UFO Encyclopedia* by John Spencer, he was quoted in 1975:

> The subject of UFOs is one that has interested me for a long time... I made an effort to find out what was in the building at Wright Patterson... I was understandably denied this request... It is still classified above top secret.

Jackie Gleason

On August 16, 1983, an article appeared in the *National Enquirer* written by Beverly Gleason, years after her husband, Jackie Gleason had died. In the article, she writes of an incident that Jackie had told her one night after returning home late at night. (The accuracy of this story is really only known to Jackie and Beverly.)

Jackie Gleason and President Nixon were very good friends and golfing buddies. One day, President Nixon, according to Gleason, had arranged for him to go to Homestead Air Force Base in Florida where he was given a heavily armed escort into the base, to a place where he saw four tables, each with a small alien body on it. The bodies had been recovered from a UFO crash. When Jackie told his wife this story, Beverly expressed a look of disbelief and was quickly given a long stare by her husband, indicating that he was telling the truth.[81]

DAN ACKROYD

Dan Ackroyd, when asked what got him started in his belief in UFOs, stated that it began when he was 8 years old and saw an article about UFOs over Washington, D.C., in 1952. Dan's interest in UFOs has earned him the position of the Hollywood consultant for the international research organization, the Mutual UFO Network.

ARTHUR GODFREY

This well known radio and television personality was also a very experienced pilot who flew for the Navy before becoming a celebrity. He always flew from his home in Virginia to New York City. During one of his personal flights from New York City to Washington, D.C., he had an encounter with a UFO. It was June 1965, and he was flying near Philadelphia with his co-pilot Frank Munciello, when a brightly lit object appeared near the right wing. He quickly banked the plane to the left, fearing a collision with the object. Then he got on the radio and called the airport to find out what was supposed to be in the air. He was told that nothing was supposed to be there. He replied, "Well there is." At this point, the object circled around the plane and came up on the other side. Frightened, Godfrey kept trying to bank his plane to get away from the object, but every time he did, the object would move right along with him. It stayed with them for a while and then just shot up into the night sky and disappeared.[82]

VICE PRESIDENT DICK CHENEY

Vice President Dick Cheney was asked during an April 2001 Washington, D.C. open line show whether he had ever been briefed on the subjects of UFOs, and if so, what he had been told. His reply seemed to put out the final embers of the UFO disclosure fire. "If I had been briefed on UFOs," replied Cheney, "it probably would have been classified, and I wouldn't be talking about it."[83]

ALIEN ABDUCTIONS

There is a huge field of literature on the subject of alien abductions. Most of it does not lie within the scope of this book, but there are a couple of incidents that involve law enforcement officers that do need to be mentioned.

Alien abduction is no different than a human abduction. It is a kidnapping and is illegal. When an alien kidnapping occurs, it usually goes unreported for various reasons. One reason is that the witness may never remember that the incident happened. All too many times, when a person is returned from the abduction, they have had the experience erased from their memory and may not ever remember it unless something happens that triggers that memory. It is the same as in human abductions, in which case, the trauma and violence causes the victim to shut out the memory. Sometimes, the trigger may be in the form of a dream of something that happens in the every day life of the abductees that, for some reason, just sits in the back of the mind and wants to come out very badly. This could be a place, an action, or one of many other things.

In an alien abduction, certain elements are common to many people's experiences. There is the abduction or the taking of a person against their will. (Sometimes the abductees will think that they are in favor of going.) The abductors (aliens) do something to the person's body. It may be in the form of rape, insertion of foreign bodies (implants) or just a physical examination. The abductees will then be returned (in almost all cases) to where they were taken from. They may not remember the incident at all or may think it was a dream. Sometimes they recall everything immediately. Their life as they have known it may change. They may not look at things the way they did before or they may fear things that they didn't prior. In this way, too, alien abduction is similar to human kidnapping.

One big difference though, is in the reporting of the abduction. Where does the abductee go? A kidnap victim can report her or his incident to the police and an investigation begins. An alien abduction victim cannot do this because it will not be believed. When a kidnap victim reports the incident, a report is filed and the search for the kidnappers begins.

The police have a description, and in most cases, a composite drawing is made of the kidnapper(s) and circulated. Try reporting to the police that you were kidnapped and sexually assaulted by little gray beings that took you away into a flying saucer. You will be met with ridicule and told to stop wasting the officers' time. Unfortunately, this is what happens, and it has happened to police officers, just as it has to the general public.

POLICE SERGEANT HERBERT SCHIRMER, ASHLAND, NEBRASKA

One such case involved Police Sergeant Herbert Schirmer in Ashland, Nebraska. On December 3, 1967, Shirmer was out on patrol around 2:30 a.m., checking out some farmlands when he noticed that a bull was acting strangely in a fenced-in field, and was charging the gate. A couple of times as he drove by, he would check the gates to make sure they were closed and locked. Satisfied that everything was all right, he continued on his patrol. He then noticed some red lights down the road that he thought might be a stopped truck, and drove over to see if there was a problem. As he approached the lights, he realized that it wasn't a truck, but was unable to identify the object. Getting closer to it, he turned on his high beams, and it took off into the sky and vanished. He later wrote in the log book, "Saw a flying saucer at the junction of highways 6 and 63. Believe it or not."

In many UFO abduction cases, this is all that is remembered of the event. However, after going home, Schirmer developed a bad headache and a buzzing noise kept him from falling asleep. This developed into a long-term problem and on February 13, 1968 Schirmer, accompanied by his Police Chief Bill Wlaskin, met with psychologist Dr. R. Leo Sprinkle from the University of Wyoming for regressive hypnosis. During this session, Schirmer recalled that when he approached the flying saucer, the engine in his patrol car went dead. There was no power at all. When he tried to call for assistance, he discovered that his radio was also dead.

Schirmer recalled that a "white blurred object had come out of the craft and mentally communicated with him." He had tried to pull out his revolver from its holster but was unable to do so. He was given some information about the craft and that he was doing a good job. He was told to not discuss this incident with anyone. When this hypnotic session was over, Schirmer and Wlaskin returned back home and he tried to go on with his life.

Even with this experience behind him, Sgt. Schirmer was soon promoted to Chief of Police when Wlaskin retired. Schirmer was only 22 years old when the sighting occurred and he became the youngest police chief in the West. However, things still weren't going well for Schirmer and he resigned his job after only two months. "I resigned because I wasn't paying attention to my job," he said. "I kept wondering about what happened that night."

Later that year, Schirmer met with another hypnotist, Loring G Williams. Williams put Schirmer through another session of hypnosis. This time more details of the incident came out. When his vehicle's power failed, the saucer had landed in the field next to him. Occupants exited from the craft and approached his car. One of the figures sprayed a greenish-like gas over the car and he was instantly paralyzed. He then found himself outside of the car standing next to one of the aliens. He described them as being about 4 ½ to 5 feet tall. They had grayish-white skin, their eyes were slanted catlike and they had flat noses and slit-like mouths. They started to ask about the area around them and pointing to a nearby power plant, asked if that was the only power source there was. They were also interested in a nearby reservoir. Schirmer thought this was all a dream until one of them squeezed his shoulder. He was taken to the craft where a circle opened up under the craft. They went into a room that Schirmer estimated to be about twenty-six feet by twenty feet. The beings seemed to be communicating telepathically and vocally. He was given a tour of the craft and told that it operated by reverse-electro magnetism. There was a crystal-like rotor in the middle of the ship and two large columns. These were reactors. Reversing electric and magnetic energy allowed them to control matter and overcome the forces of gravity. The craft could draw electricity from power lines and they also drew power from water. He was instructed not to tell anyone about this experience and told that he would be contacted two more times. He was returned to his car and he remembered nothing that happened. The whole incident lasted only about twenty minutes.[84]

THE TRUE STORY OF THE BROOKLYN BRIDGE UFO ABDUCTIONS

In his book, *Witnessed*, Budd Hopkins relates the true experience of a woman in Brooklyn, New York City, who was abducted from her apartment near the Brooklyn Bridge by small creatures during the middle of the night. The book's title indicates that the story is not only about the abductees, but also about those who watched the event and how their lives intertwined with those of the participants.

The primary witnesses of the abduction were NYPD officers who were working security detail for a major world political leader who was also in the car. Sitting under the FDR Drive at 3 a.m., on November 30, 1989, they saw the woman floating from her window up to a UFO along a blue beam of light, accompanied by small creatures. The two police officers later contacted her to find out what had happened and why. As others who were there that night began to come forward, it became clear that many were not only witnesses, but abductees as well.[85]

FRANK SORIANO'S PERSONAL EXPERIENCES

I'd never set out to become a UFO statistic, or to witness even one UFO, let alone all of the ones I remember seeing over the years. I was born in Puerto Rico and was raised in Spanish Harlem in New York City. I married my childhood sweetheart and just wanted to raise a family and live a normal life. However, fate was not going to allow it. I have lived in New York City, Yonkers, Ticonderoga, and the town of Wilton, all in New York state, and have had UFO sightings in every area I have lived. They are not always the same type of craft. I have seen triangular shapes, saucer-shaped crafts, tubular- or peanut-shaped crafts, round-shaped crafts, and oblong-shaped crafts. Below is a representative, not complete, list of sightings that have plagued me for most of my life.

BRONX, NEW YORK – 1978

On the weekend evening of August 26, 1978, in Yonkers, New York, my cousin, Willie, and I were looking forward to a weekend jaunt to a Brooklyn pool hall for games, beer, and some laughter on a hot summer night of fun.

Willie's wife, Annette, would stay with my wife Miriam, in Yonkers. Both Miriam and Annette were not very happy about Willie and me going into Brooklyn. Both of them worried about all of the crime in the city. Willie and I assured them not to worry and that we would be fine. Little did we ever dream that an event would occur that night that would change our way of thinking and the thought process instilled in us since childhood, and would alter our lives forever.

Willie suggested that I drive my car so he could relax as the passenger and soak up the summer night sights without the distraction of driving in traffic. I did not mind, as I enjoyed the challenge of driving on the New York City highways.

I moved onto the Major Deegan Highway heading south toward Brooklyn with the car windows wide open, taking in the breeze. We were both excited about getting together with family and friends, and to having a good time playing pool and drinking beer.

We drove past Fordham Road joking and laughing. We saw a sign up ahead indicating the George Washington Bridge. On the right-hand side of the highway were two tall high-rise apartment buildings about a quarter of a mile ahead of us. At this point, I noticed a group of large white lights that appeared to be attached to the top of one of the buildings near the highway sticking out as though it were a neon sign. It was two horizontal rows of large round white lights. Each row had six lights, one row above the other.

I mentioned to Willie, "Hey Cuz, look up there at the top of that building. It looks like they're putting up a neon sign." Willie said that it looked weird.

Suddenly, all of the lights began moving in unison as though affixed to a solid structure. It was as if it had just detached itself from the top floor of the high-rise building at a moderate rate of speed, moving straight as though it were on a track and stopping suddenly above the moving traffic on the highway below it. We both looked at it for a moment in stunned silence.

The gray-haired older man behind the wheel of the car to my left nearly collided with me as he too observed this incredible sight. I snapped him out of it by honking my horn.

This craft, or whatever it was, stopped sharply above the highway and hung there without a flicker like it was sitting on a shelf. It remained silent and still as I drove under and past it. Willie immediately jumped into the back seat to see it from the back window. The craft then moved back toward the building and around it as if scanning it. I looked at my watch and noted that the time was 9:45 p.m.

This incident made such an impact on our emotional and mental status that it changed forever how we looked at life and its mysteries. Whatever this object was, we knew that it was not of human origin. The lights were so bright we could not see the shape of the craft.

The idea of a fun-filled evening of beer and pool with family and friends quickly changed to a late night (and early morning) discussion of the UFO and what it could *not* be, such as an airplane, helicopter, blimp, or balloon. We both just sat in front of Willie's mother's home drinking beer, talking, and pondering the amazing sight we'd both witnessed, along with possibly countless number of others who must have also witnessed the same UFO hovering about twenty stories up in the air.

My belief in UFOs began that night at 9:45 p.m., August 26, 1978, in the Bronx in New York City.

0 0 0

SING SING PRISON 1984 OR 1985

Sing Sing Prison sits right on the shore of the Hudson River in Ossining, New York. This "Castle on the Hudson," as it was known, is about thirty miles north of New York City. The prison is known throughout the world as a notorious home for some of the most vicious criminals such as the Rosenbergs, the A-bomb spies and Louis Lepke, the head of Murder Inc.

One night, in the summer of 1985, an event occurred that shattered old beliefs and instilled some new ones for both employees and inmates at the prison. I was on duty that night, assigned to Building 7, the inmate honor block. As I went about my duties, I could hear radio transmissions, officers' voices crackling through the prison. Suddenly, one radio unit called out to all available units to be advised that a very large object was approaching the facility by air. Other units began transmitting that they, too, had the object under observation. It was described as huge and crescent-shaped, with blinking red, blue, and green lights underneath it, moving east at a very slow pace. It was silent and had no wings.

One voice asked Tower 3, which faced east, overlooking the train tracks at the main part of the prison, if he had it in sight. The reply was affirmative. Another unit asked if the watch commander had been notified yet. As the object moved over Tower 15, a voice then asked if anyone was going to submit a report on this. The responses were almost all the same. "Negative, negative, hell no."

Later, I spoke to a few of the other officers about the incident. Only one person was willing to discuss it with me, and only briefly. No one wanted to report it, much less even talk about it. One officer told me, "I can tell you this, that thing ain't ours, it looked like nothing I've ever seen. Man, it was silent and seemed almost as big as the prison. Man, I don't want to deal with this &%$#. The officer of Tower 3 won't talk about it with anyone, he'll deny anything ever happened so don't bother to ask."

DRESDEN, NEW YORK - 1993

On a rainy autumn night, a little past midnight on November 8, 1993, I had just been relieved from my third shift tour by the midnight to eight shift at Great Meadows Correctional Facility. My wife, Miriam, had finished the three to eleven shift already. As usual, she was sitting in the car waiting for me to join her and head for home to Ticonderoga, a thirty-two-mile trip through rural mountainous Adirondack, New York State.

We only made a quick stop in Whitehall at a convenience store to pick up some Half and Half for our morning coffee. We got back on the road and continued home as the steady rain fell from the very dark sky. By the time we were about halfway home, Miriam was watching the flickering reflections of our headlights on the wet tree branches as we drove by them.

Suddenly, Miriam told me to look over to a mountain slightly ahead and to the right. It was Spruce Mountain, on the state line between New York and Vermont, along the Champlain Canal. In the entire seven years that we had lived in Ticonderoga and traveled to and from work along this road, we had never seen any lights on this mountain until now.

As we rounded the curve and the area opened out, Miriam cried out, "Oh my God!"

Spruce Mountain location where Frank and Miriam Soriano saw a UFO. The artist rendition (by Frank) gives the reader an idea of the size and look of the UFO craft. The circled area, on the full-scene photo, is the approximate location of the craft as it was seen with the mountain backdrop. *Courtesy Frank Soriano.*

There in front of us on top of Spruce Mountain was a huge object. (The photograph is the witness's rendition of the mountain and object. The tops of the trees and the sky is blackened out so that you can see the position of the craft.) Its length was incredible, its height about thirty to forty feet. There were two rows, one above the other, of what appeared to be windows, each one larger than several SUVs. The outside of the craft and the windows were lit with an amber-colored light. The light was bright, but strangely contained to the craft itself, and did not light up the area around it.

I was truly fascinated by this craft and pulled over to the side of the road. The wipers kept clearing the windshield of the rain drops, clearly showing that huge craft just hovering above the tree tops on the mountain. I opened my driver's side window and briefly stuck my head outside. It was still raining but I could see the object clearly.

"It is real!" I said to Miriam, but I was not sure she heard me. I brought my head back into the car and wiped the rain-water off my face. The cold water had convinced me that I was not dreaming or imagining this. Miriam opened her window as well, and agreed that the object was real.

Wanting to get a better view of the object, I turned the car around, drove back about fifty feet to a point higher and made another U-turn. I pulled the car over to the side of the road and parked the car to get a better view of the object. We sat there and just stared at the object. I have never seen anything so big before. Miriam said that it was time to leave, but I told her to wait. I was fixated by this craft and overwhelmed by fascination. I didn't want to leave. I felt a little nervous, but overwhelmed by curiosity, I stayed and stared.

I decided to turn off the headlights and the engine so that Miriam and I could see the craft in total darkness. When the lights and engine were off, the sight was just magnificent. The light of the craft was the only light in the entire area.

Suddenly, the amber lights on the craft began to dim. Frantically, Miriam shouted, "They've seen us, they know we're here!"

I tried to calm her and said, "Let's wait a minute."

Panicking, she screamed, "Damn it, they've seen us! They know we are here! Let's get the $%!# out of here!" Her face was streaked with tears. She began punching me with a clenched fist, yelling, "We have to leave, we have to leave now!"

I saw terror in my wife's eyes. It reminded me of the scene in the movie *Jaws*, when the girl was swimming and was pulled under by the shark. She briefly broke the surface of the water, her head tilted back and her mouth wide open. This was the look on Miriam's face as she blindly punched at me, begging me to leave. It was as if she knew something that I didn't know, and it terrified her.

Miriam is not easily frightened. She and I grew up together, and Miriam has stood up to four muggers with knives and saved my life after they had knocked me out. In her work as a corrections officer, she has faced down some of the biggest and meanest of prisoners. I have never in my life seen Miriam display any fear until now. It affected me deeply, and I started the engine and took her home.

As we drove, Miriam trembled and did not want to talk about the incident. She just sat looking out the window without making any sound other than occasional sniffles. The sight that we just witnessed was just unbelievable. But, it was real and that was what makes this incident so intimidating and awe-inspiring.

I phoned UFO investigator Paul Bartholomew, in Whitehall, New York. We later met at the site where Miriam and I had sat in the car and watched the object. Miriam refused to go with us or to talk about it. Paul told me that there had been other UFO reports made at the same time that night. I later got in touch with MUFON, met with Jim Bouck and Ray Cecot, MUFON investigators, and filed a UFO report with them. Miriam still would not talk about it.

Ticonderoga, New York – 1998

While Miriam and I were doing some yard work at around 8 p.m. the evening of July, 2 1998, we watched an object fly silently across the sky. When I first saw it, I ran into the house to grab my video camera and was able to get about 12.5 seconds of video of the object. As I ran into the house, Miriam looked up to see what had me excited and watched the object till it vanished behind a cloud. As it moved across the sky, it vanished behind a building on my property. I moved quickly to go behind the house to continue videotaping. As I approached the rear of the building, my steps slowed and I felt a loss of interest. I then returned the camera to its case in the house.

Frank and Mirium Soriano during the time frame of the Ticonderoga, New York (1998) sighting.

I did not remember the event that evening, and didn't realize what had happened until eight days later, when I finally realized that Miriam and I never discussed the sighting until July 10. Miriam and I then began to question what had happened and why we'd never discussed the event until eight days later. That was when we sat and looked at the videotape for the first time.

The object on the video was capsule (pill) shaped. MUFON analyst Dr. Bruce Maccabee analyzed the videotape. He was able to rule out the possibility of a blimp and airplane. The final result of the analysis was that of an unidentified flying object. The object matched the description of one that was seen in the same county a year earlier, by three other witnesses which was investigated by Jim Bouck.

Also, this appears to be the same object that was seen by the Russian Cosmonaut Vladmir Kovalyonok. When analyzing my sighting and video, Dr. Maccabee mentioned to me that he thought he could see blue sky in between the object at the center as though they could separate into two objects. This may be supported by the sightings of the similar objects seen by the Russian Cosmonaut and by the police chief in Lagrange, Georgia.

One thing is certain: they have been observed in orbit outside our atmosphere. During the mid-1970s a young Russian Cosmonaut in orbit aboard the Soyuz observed a UFO as two oval objects moving in unison as one structure. He then watched them separate into two UFOs and move into different directions. This Cosmonaut is now Lt. General Vladmir Kovalyonok. His drawing of the UFO appears exactly like the Ticonderoga, New York UFO I saw and videotaped.

On October 17, 1993, as the space shuttle *Columbia STS-58* was entering orbit at approximately 222,000 feet, NASA film footage caught an object moving past the shuttle at a very high speed. Examination of individual frames of the film footage reveals two oval objects moving past the shuttle as one unit with what appears to be a dark line in the center of it, similar to the Ticonderoga UFO.

A copy of the video analysis of my video by Dr. Bruce Maccabee can be seen in the appendix section of this book.

JIM BOUCK'S UFO SIGHTING
...ABOUT FRANK AND MIRIAM

I have known Frank and Miriam since about 1993 when I responded to a request from Frank to investigate and look into a UFO sighting that he and Miriam had over Spruce Mountain on their way home from work. Frank and I got along well and we kept in touch quite frequently through the years. I responded to every sighting that he had and never once did I feel that he was making any of it up. I always knew that there was something more to his sightings besides the sightings themselves. I would ask him every time if he remembered everything and if he might have had any missing time. It would have been easy for him to say yes even if he was hoaxing something, but he would tell me no or he doesn't know. As the years went by, he began to respond that he wasn't sure. Maybe, but he couldn't recall it or he didn't think so.

We would talk for hours sometimes and he would tell me everything that he could recall. Frank has a fantastic memory of details and dates and times. Never did he change anything and I would question him many times and in different order. For a long time, Frank never wanted his name to be known. In early reports, he would be known by a pseudonym. Frank would tell nobody of what had happened except for a very few friends and family members. He valued his anonymity. As the years went by and he knew he was seeing more UFOs than should be normal for most witnesses and he'd also retired from his State Correctional job, Frank decided to, as he would put it "come out of the UFO closet."

Miriam still did not want anybody to know what had been happening to her and would not discuss it. Frank no longer cared who knew. This took a lot of courage to take a stand like this. As other researchers began to look into his experiences, such as Budd Hopkins, Dr. Bruce Macabbee, and Stanton Friedman as well as others, Frank never changed his story or embellished it. He didn't need to.

Miriam had accepted what was happening to her, but she still didn't have the strength Frank did in standing up for his experiences. This does not make Miriam any less a strong person. She has gone through a lot since she realized what was happening and she has accepted more than most UFO witnesses dare to accept.

0 0 0

Now, Frank and Miriam are going another step into the view of the world by standing up for their past in this book. Frank has never backed down from anybody whether it was during his law enforcement days or his UFO experiences, and he is going to stand tall in this.

It Was My Turn

When I had my own first sighting, I wasn't sure if it was actually a UFO. I was taking a nap in my back yard on a lounge chair and had just woken up. I looked up at the sky, picked up and put on my eyeglasses and looked to the East. I thought I saw an object that looked like what Frank had been seeing, but I couldn't trust my eyes because I wasn't really focused yet. The object left and I decided to try to watch more carefully more often from the yard.

I'd already determined that it might be possible to see the object from my yard after having looked at a map and seeing that the sightings Frank had, had formed a pattern and followed a path that I hoped would be visible from my home. Frank first saw this object from his home in Ticonderoga, New York. It had also been seen in the same county a year earlier by someone else and in Vermont by a UFO researcher. When Frank had moved to Saratoga County he continued seeing the object moving either Southwest to Northeast or Northeast to Southwest as it did in Ticonderoga. Drawing a line on the map from Vermont where a UFO investigator had his own sighting of the same object, through Ticonderoga and Saratoga County, I was able to see that the object seemed to go south through either part of Schenectady or Albany County. It was along this path that I was able to see it. This time I had with me a 35mm camera with a 200 mm telephoto lens. I shot a number of photos of the object and then had the film developed. It looked exactly as the object in Frank's photos.

I had now been able to confirm that the object was continuing to move further South in its travel. Now I had proof that I had finally seen a UFO. Using information from interviews and investigative techniques, I had in a way tracked one down and been able to witness it. I was able to use information I learned and recorded to determine a path and follow a pattern. I would not have been able to do this had it not been for Frank, whose constant watching of the sky and continued sighting of the object, giving me the information needed. I believe that others can do this also if there is some sort of pattern that can be determined from a number of sightings in any area.

As I had mentioned earlier in the book, I lived and worked as a police officer in the Hudson Valley area at the beginning of what was to become one of the biggest UFO flaps in the country and the history of Ufology. I never did get to see a UFO at that time, but now, with the help of Frank, I have seen my first UFO. Hopefully, it was not my last.

Fire Fighter's Guide to Disaster Control and UFOs

Since this book is about law enforcement officers, we want discuss another emergency service's response to this phenomena. Many emergencies require the collaboration of several responders.

The fire department is required to be at many types of emergencies in addition to fire calls, including accidents, hazardous materials, search and rescue, and many more. Law enforcement officers and firefighters work hand in hand in many situations. In some cases, especially in rural areas, the law enforcement officer may be a volunteer fireman also. The Fire Fighter's Guide To Disaster Control is used to train fire fighters, and contained a chapter on preparing for the possibility of an UFO encounter. This chapter was only in the 1993 edition of this book, and has since been removed from subsequent editions.

The book was written by William Kramer and Charles Bahme. It is written every year for fire companies, departments, and fire academies throughout the United States. It is distributed throughout the country through the United States Fire Administration, a division of the Department of Homeland Security's Federal Emergency Management Agency.

In the text, the authors explain that the reason this subject has been added to the manual was not so much due to a particular incident, but more to the perceived threat that may happen if the enigma of UFOs and the potentiality of an attack should happen. They discussed what happened in 1938 when Orson Welles presented his radio show War of the Worlds. Many people tuning into the radio broadcast after it had started did not hear the announcement that it was just a radio show and they thought that they were listening to a real news broadcast of an alien attack. Panic swept throughout the entire listening area.

They wanted to prepare firefighters for the potential disasters of such an occurrence due to the disruption of services, panic, and safety concerns. Should such an attack happen, the police agencies, rescue, and fire departments should be aware of what they are dealing with and what to expect. An example might be the from the 1996 movie *Independence Day* starring Will Smith.

Another reason for presenting this chapter in the manual was because a precedent had been made in 1959 when the Inspector General of the United State Air Force had issued an Operation and Training Order, "Unidentified Flying Objects – sometimes treated lightly by the press and referred to as 'Flying Saucers'– must be rapidly and accurately identified as serious Air Force business..." This was done even though the Air Force maintained to the public that UFOs were no threat to the U.S.

This UFO disaster chapter was also written years after President Ronald Reagan had discussions with Russian General Secretary Mikhail Gorbachev and his famous speech before the United Nations about how the countries of the world should try to work together for the good of the planet in the event of an alien attack from space. Also discussed was the suspected attack by aliens on the city of Los Angeles in 1942 shortly after the attack on Pearl Harbor, as mentioned earlier in this book. It was thought by some that the attack on Los Angeles was from the Russians or the Japanese, but years later it was documented that these countries had nothing to do with the attack.

Kramer and Brahme then go into the history of Ufology and the alleged sightings, UFO crashes, the 1965 blackout over the entire Eastern Seaboard, including the reports of UFOs causing it. Mentioned also were the attempts that the United States Air Force went through to discourage reports and witnesses.

They discussed the potential hazards of a UFO landing and attack with the possibility of powerful electrical fields and the psychological effects that it would have on the general population. The authors also list the potential that the UFO occupants have in the disruption of air and ground traffic and the control that they display in stopping vehicles, radios, and other things from operating.

For the reason of being under the control of a government agency, the future training books after this one have all left out any reference to UFOs, the potential dangers from them and what needs to be known by future emergency responders. You can find the entire chapter by doing a computer search for The Fire Fighter's Guide To Disaster Control.

Fire Engineering Books and Videos, 1992
Made available to fire departments and fire academies throughout
the United States by the U.S. Fire Administration (USFA),
An entity of the Department of Homeland Security's Federal
Emergency Management Agency

CONCLUSION

For a number of years, certain questions have recurred concerning the origin of UFO crafts. Are they solid objects that travel through space, are they interdimensional crafts, or are they from here on Earth? They may be all three, or something else altogether.

One thing is certain: They have been observed in orbit outside our atmosphere. During the mid-1970s, a young Russian Cosmonaut in orbit aboard the Soyuz observed a UFO as two oval objects moving in unison as one structure. He then watched them separate into two UFOs and move into different directions. This Cosmonaut is now Lt. General Vladmir Kovalyonok. As mentioned earlier, his drawing of the UFO appears exactly like the Ticonderoga, New York UFO seen and videotaped by Frank Soriano.

On October 17, 1993, as the space shuttle *Columbia STS-58* was entering orbit at approximately 222,000 feet, NASA film footage caught an object moving past the shuttle at a very high speed. Examination of individual frames of the film footage reveals two oval objects moving past the shuttle as one unit with what appears to be a dark line in the center of it, similar to the Ticonderoga UFO.

These sightings are not imaginary. Many occur during broad daylight, when the witnesses are wide awake. How can you videotape a flying craft of unknown origin crossing the sky in broad daylight and be able to zoom in on it, follow it with the camera and be able to capture images on film, if this is all a dream or a delusion? How can the debunkers explain that away? Rest assured, they will find a way. But their refusal to face facts, no matter how steadfast they may be, does not change reality or our need to deal with it.

We all know about "them," the UFOs and their pilots. We know, our wives know, our children know, our friends know, millions of people know, some of the best minds on Earth know. Our government knows, although they will not acknowledge it. Although we all know, we still need that stamp of approval from our government in order to get facts released that will help us understand and deal with our reality.

Many have asked, if there are UFOs and aliens visiting us, why haven't they stopped at the White House? This is a good question. The President of the United States has a lot of clout and would be the one with the most to be able to give to any foreign visiting dignitaries. Every foreign leader who comes to the U.S. visits the President. It is a gesture of good will and they are always looking for something. Usually, it's some way to make relations better and to promote peace between the two nations. What better way to iron out differences than to sit down and discuss face-to-face how to make or keep the peace?

The impact of a space craft and its occupants landing on the White House lawn would be tremendous. Media from all over the world would be there to document it. Crowds would fill up every inch of space they could to try and get a glimpse of it, as in the movie, *The Day The Earth Stood Still*. By doing this, the aliens would definitely get noticed. They would be able to come out from hiding. No more sneaking around at night or hiding in deep waters or mountainous forests. Then, there is also the chance to stay in the Lincoln bedroom for the night.

So why wouldn't they stop in at the White House? Why should they? What would they gain by it? Chatting with the President doesn't guarantee that they would be able to do what they want to do without any objections or restrictions. If a zoologist were to encounter a new species of animal in the jungle, would they go to the head of a herd to seek permission to take one of the animals for study? If one of our astronauts landing on another planet were to encounter an alien race, would he insist on meeting with the leader of that race before studying them and learning all they could about them? Before a person swats and kills a bee, does he find the Queen bee first and let her know what the intentions are? Many people fear that if these beings can get here from their home, wherever that may be, then they have the intelligence and ability to do just about anything thing they want to. So why would they bother to ask us for permission?

Are we being visited? Could it be that all of the people who say that they have seen a UFO are being truthful, and honest? Probably not. People do sometimes look for a way to make a buck, to get attention, or just to have fun at someone else's expense. But not everyone. Polls indicate that most people are telling the truth, describing to the best of their knowledge and ability, the amazing things they have seen. The job of the investigator is to try to determine who fits in which group, the honest witness or the one who is either dishonest or deluded.

Although some witnesses see only one UFO in their lives, others have seen many. Some witnesses have recalled seeing something at a very young age and many more times as he or she has grown up. Some may have even had other experiences along with the sighting. These sightings and experiences may not be recalled immediately, but the memory usually filters through later in life, sometimes as a dream or a flashback.

Many witnesses have discovered that their family members, such as sons and daughters, have also had many sightings. It seems to run in some families, especially if abduction is involved.

Witnesses come in all sizes, shapes, colors, backgrounds, and so forth. The important aspect in all of them is their credibility.

The objects described in this book may or may not be alien crafts. We can only go by the testimony of the witnesses, whom we believe we have identified as very credible people. The sworn word of any of these men and women would be accepted by a court of law, by the media, and by governmental officials under any other circumstance. However, since they are reporting something that the public finds difficult to accept, their testimony is ignored.

These sightings are not only being reported by law enforcement officers, but also by military and civilian pilots, scientists, politicians, and people from all walks of life. Yet our government continues to deny the existence of these crafts, even though they have been caught on film by government agencies such as NASA and the military itself. This continuous lie and cover up based on ignorance and deceit will result in severe consequences in the future. These UFOs are here for a reason not yet known to us. What awaits us? The ignorance of consequence is the consequence of ignorance.

If all of these people are crazy, seeing things that aren't there, then we are a doomed planet because this is a worldwide phenomenon. These sightings have been going on throughout recorded history, beginning long before we began paying attention to it in 1947.

We need to keep an open mind. Don't be afraid to accept what you see, or to question it. If you see an object or an unusual light in the sky, tell someone about it. You may be surprised to find out that others have seen it and were afraid to say anything. Such was the case with Frank Soriano. He has had numerous sightings in his life, and kept most of them to himself or shared them only with Miriam. When he dared to open up and start telling friends and colleagues, he found out that he was not alone.

There are still so many questions to be answered. Some people may know the truth and are afraid to share it. We can understand why they feel that way, but if they can be inspired by the courage of these law enforcement officers who have come forward, more witnesses standing together can only give more support to those who are still afraid to step up. It will lend them the courage to make themselves heard, to let their friends, relatives, and the public in general know what they know, and to help them face the truth about what is happening in the world today.

A REQUEST TO OUR BROTHERS AND SISTERS IN LAW ENFORCEMENT

We have a request for all members of Law Enforcement. In this book you have seen the testimony of law enforcement members from all over the world. We have only touched the surface. If one person sees a UFO, probably more have seen it also, but are intimidated and scared to come forward. We ask that you stand up and be counted like your brothers and sisters in law enforcement and let everyone know what you have seen. Maybe it can be explained, maybe not. But stand up and be counted. We, Frank and Jim, ask that you contact us with your experience. Did you see something and or experience something unusual?

Email us at nitesiter@yahoo.com with your story. Let us know. If you are willing to be known, let us put your name and picture (in uniform) and document your experience in our next book.

A closed mind is a blindness of reason and possibilities.

~Frank Soriano

TRIBUTE TO THE PIONEERS OF THE UFO ENIGMA

We would like to thank those individuals who have led the way to the enlightenment of this subject by acknowledging their research, investigations, and sacrifices. As pioneers in the study and analysis of UFO and their pilots, their many years of investigations and research have made them the experts of the field. They went forth and spoke of this subject that many knew little about and were afraid to pursue, while others mocked it without any effort to understand.

Thank you to the following for taking a stand and leading us in our interests and working for our knowledge: Stanton Friedman, Budd Hopkins, Bruce Maccabee, Dennis Anderson, Leo Sprinkle, Walt Andrus, Richard Dolan, David Jacobs, Leonard Stringfield, Kenneth Arnold, Jim and Coral Lorenzen, Maj. Donald Keyhoe, and John Mack.

The questions related to UFOs may not be answered today, they may not be answered tomorrow; but they will one day be answered due to the efforts of these pioneers.

APPENDIX

FLYING PEANUT OR DOUBLE UFO?
BY
BRUCE MACCABEE

July 2, 1998. A quiet Thursday evening in Ticonderoga, New York (population about 3,500 – 4,000). Fred and Mary (pseudonyms; witnesses requested anonymity) were in their yard. Mary was working in the garden while Fred was watering plants. It was about 8 p.m. when he decided he needed a short break and put down the hose. He walked over to the driveway and stretched while looking up at the partly cloudy sky in the southeast. Then he saw it. He didn't know what it was, but he was immediately struck by the fact that he could not see any wings. He watched closely. No noise, either.

Suddenly it dawned on him: maybe it was a UFO! He ran into his house to get the video camera which he keeps loaded and ready to use. Mary heard the door slam behind Fred as he entered the house. She looked toward the house to see what was going on. About ten seconds later she saw him running out the door with the video camera ready to operate. He pointed the camera upward, spotted the object through the lens and started videotaping. Mary looked in the direction the camera was pointing and she, too, saw the object traveling northward through the sky east of them. She walked over toward him and stood there watching as he got about 12 1/2 seconds of video before the object disappeared above a cloud. Fred walked to another location to see if it might come out of the cloud but...no luck. That was it. The sighting had lasted, perhaps, twenty-five to thirty seconds, maximum.

About a week later, Fred was wondering who to tell about this event. He managed to locate Stanton Friedman and a local MUFON investigator, Jim Bouck. Fred sent a copy of his video to Stanton who then recommended that he call me, which he did on July 31. Subsequently he sent me his "affadavit" which recounted the history of the event and the original video for analysis. Fred wrote about their sighting as follows:

> (We) observed an object in flight moving through the clouds (and) blue sky (between clouds) from south to north. The craft was soundless and wingless and flew at a fairly fast rate of speed. The cloud ceiling level was 5,000 feet and (the object was) viewed at a 65-degree angle.

It flew on the eastern side (of Ticonderoga, New York) past St. Mary's Church. (My wife) viewed it with the naked eye and said it resembled a peanut, contoured some (i.e., narrowing down) in the center with a vertical black band or (vertical) line around the center portion of the object and that she could hear no sound from it, nor did it have any wings. We both saw it as cream or beige in color. I also didn't see wings or hear any sound coming from it. That's the reason why I quickly ran into my house to get my video camera."

The whole sighting took about a minute.

TECHNICAL ANALYSIS

The MUFON investigation determined that Fred first saw the object coming from the southeast at an azimuth of about 125 degrees. It was last seen at an azimuth of about 65 degrees. It took 25 - 30 seconds to cover this angular distance.

The analysis described below indicates that either there was a single object with a very small (so small as to be unresolved by the video) structure connecting two larger white structures or else there were two objects with the second traveling at a fixed spacing close behind the first.

There is no clear evidence in the video imagery of a connection between the white images. However, since the resolution isn't good enough to prove, there was no such connection, I refer herein to "the object(s)" in the singular, thereby allowing for either possibility.

The video begins with a wide angle view that shows the object(s) as a faint white dot in the sky, above thin clouds. The initial scene also shows Fred's house at the left and, to the right of his house, the steeple of St. Mary's Church (see Figure 1, the first frame from the original video; the circle at the right end of the track indicates the location of the image of the object(s)).

The object(s) had passed its point of closest approach to the witnesses and was already traveling away when he began videotaping. During the first several seconds, Fred zoomed in on the object(s) and then he followed it as it moved to his left (north) past the cross on top of the church. After a few seconds it disappeared in the clouds just before it reached the edge of the roof of his house. The complete track of the object(s) recorded on video is a straight line about 10 degrees in length, as illustrated in Figure 1. The object(s) was optimally illuminated by the

sun which was low in the west northwest at the time. Fred obtained about 378 frames of which about five dozen have images clear enough for analysis. For most of the other frames either the camera is out of focus, there is too much motion blur or the object(s) is lost in the clouds.

FIGURE 1

FRAME 1

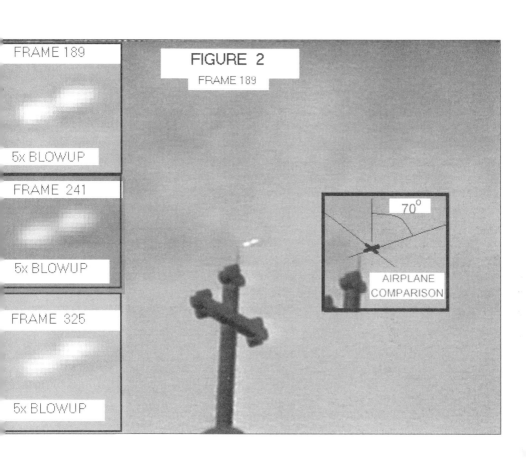

FRAME 189

5x BLOWUP

FRAME 241

5x BLOWUP

FRAME 325

5x BLOWUP

FIGURE 2

FRAME 189

70°

AIRPLANE
COMPARISON

Two Whitish Elliptical Images

Figure 2 shows the object(s) just before it passed the top of the cross on the church steeple at an azimuth of about 70 degrees. The overall image consists of two whitish elliptical or ovoid images "end to end" with a darker space between them. This gap is more easily seen in the blowup inset which was extracted from a frame in the original video that occurred a few seconds after the object(s) passed the steeple. Blowups of the clearest images show that the two white ellipses are separated by a very small distance and that between the elliptical images there is, what certainly appears to be, blue sky. Although there is no video evidence indicating a structure connecting the two ellipses, the image resolution is not sufficient to rule out the possibility of a narrow connecting structure between them. Because the white images are somewhat brighter than the blue sky, the gap between them appears as a dark area or vertical dark line even though the area actually is a pale blue color (probably a result of the white images "bleeding into" the blue sky color in the gap). The two white ellipses traveled close together without changing the spacing between them. This explains why Fred's wife had the impression that there was a single object, narrow at the center, and with a dark vertical line separating the front and back sections.

MUFON On-Scene Measurements

The steeple is at an azimuth of about 70 degrees (east northeast). The top of the cross was about 140 feet above the camera and about 267 feet away horizontally, according to measurements made by Fred and MUFON investigator Jim Bouck. Thus the angular elevation of the top of the cross was about 28 degrees. Fred obtained the airport weather information for Glens Falls, New York.

This showed about 20% sky cover at 5,000 feet, ground level visibility of 15 miles and zero wind speed. The object(s) was occasionally partially obscured and at other times completely obscured by thin clouds and ultimately was lost to view as it passed into or beyond a cloud its altitude was at least 5,000 feet. Hence the radial distance from the camera as it passed the cross was at least 5,000/sin(28) = 10,700 ft.

CAMERA CALIBRATION
AND SIZE ESTIMATE

At my request, Fred provided zoomed images of a yardstick at 69 feet. This allowed me to determine the angular size calibration. The analysis was done using computer-grabbed images from the original videotape of the object(s) and of the yardstick, for which distances are measured in pixels. At full zoom the yardstick image is 448 pixels long. The angular size of the yardstick at 69 feet is 0.0434 radians or 2.49 degrees (0.01745 radians per degree) so the angle per pixel is 9.75E-5 rad or 5.56E-3 deg. (This corresponds to an effective focal length of 10,256 pixels. Exponential notation is used: 1E0 = 1.0, 2.5E1 = 25.0, 1E2 = 100, 1E-1 = 0.1, etc.) As the object(s) passed the top of the cross, its overall length was about 19 (+/-)1 pixels measured along the slanted axis (connecting the centers) of the elliptical image in Frame 189 (Figure 2). This corresponds to (1.85 +/- 0.1)E-3 rad in angular length. The overall length of any object, as projected onto a plane perpendicular to the sighting line (a plane parallel to the focal plane), is the product of the distance to the object and the angular size of its image as measured in radians (a good approximation for angles less than 10 degrees). At a distance of 10,700 feet along the sighting line, the projected length of the image corresponds to 10,700 x (1.85 +/- 0.1)E-3 = 20 +/- 1 ft. (If the object(s) were above cloud altitude the projected length would be larger than this.)

Because the image actually appears as two elliptical white areas that may be disconnected, a dimension more applicable to these images is the spacing of their centers. In Frame 189, this is about 9.5 pixels or 9.3E-4 radians. At 10,700 feet, this corresponds to a projected spacing distance of about 10 feet. Thus if these were two elliptical objects flying along, each was about 4 feet in radius and they were traveling with a spacing of only a couple of feet. Of course, if the distance had been greater, then these dimensions also would be greater.

The length just presented is not the actual length of the object(s) since it was viewed at an oblique angle. (This is the length as projected onto a plane parallel to the focal plane.) It is now necessary to estimate the actual length.

ORIENTATION ASSUMPTION
AND ESTIMATE OF LENGTH

The actual length can be calculated only if one makes an assumption about the orientation in space of the major axis of the object(s). I have chosen to assume the major axis was horizontal and that the object(s) traveled in a horizontal plane at a constant altitude, although I could not rule out the possibility that it traveled upward or downwards at a small angle. With this "horizontal assumption" the tilt angle, b, of the axis of the image (connecting the centers) relative to vertical on the focal plane and the angle of elevation, e, of the sighting line can be combined to calculate the angle, a, between the horizontal axis of the object and the (horizontal) azimuth of the sighting line. The angle, a, is measured in a horizontal plane at the altitude of the object(s) by performing a counterclockwise rotation (as seen from above) starting in the direction of the sighting azimuth and ending in the direction of the axis of the object(s). The formula for calculating a is a = arctan[(tan b)(sin e)], where b is measured relative to a vertical line on the image plane that passes through the image by starting at vertical and rotating clockwise "down" to the axis of the image. In this case b is about 70 deg (see insert in Figure 2) and e = 28 deg so a = 52 deg. Since the azimuth of the steeple, 70 deg, is measured clockwise from north and angle a is measured counterclockwise from the sighting azimuth, the axis of this object(s) had an azimuth of 70-52 = 17 deg relative to north. Since the track of the object(s) as illustrated in Figure 1 aligns with the axis of the object(s), it was traveling almost due north.

Using angles a and e, the actual overall length of the object(s) can be calculated from the projected length, 20 feet, again assuming that the object(s) axis lies in a horizontal plane. This is accomplished by dividing the projected length by a projection factor which is the square root of ([sin a]^2 + [cos a]^2 x [sin e]^2), where "^2" means "squared." With a = 52 and e = 28 this factor is the square root of 0.70 which is 0.84. Hence the projected length should be divided by 0.84: 20/.84 = 24 feet (comparable to but smaller than a Piper Cherokee Lance or Beechcraft Model 76, singengine propellor driven). The height of the object(s), allowing for the natural diffuseness of the edges of the elliptical images, appears to be about 1/5 or 1/4 of the overall length, i.e., about 4 to 6 feet if at an altitude of 5,000 feet. Similarly, the centers of the white images were separated by 10 feet/0.84 which is about 12 feet if at an altitude of 5,000 feet.

Size Variation with Assumed Altitude

The object(s) was occasionally partially obscured and occasionally totally obscured by the clouds. This means that the object(s) could have been at cloud height (5,000 feet) or above. If above, then the calculated size would be larger.

For example, if it were assumed to have been at 10,000 feet altitude, the range would have been 21,400 feet (4 miles) and the overall length would be about 48 feet (comparable in size to a business jet [Gates Learjet] or fighter aircraft [e.g., Grumman A-6E]); if at 15,000 feet, then it would have been 6 miles away and about 72 feet long; if at 32,000 feet it would have been about 12 miles away and about 145 feet long (comparable to a Boeing 707).

Estimated Speed

The object(s) passed behind the lightning rod at the top of the cross. It required 4 frames (at 30 frames/second) or 4/30 = 2/15 of a second to pass the lightning rod. If it were about 24 feet in length this would correspond to about 180 feet/second or about 123 MPH. If it had been twice as high its speed would have been about 246 MPH, and so on for other assumed heights. At a height of 32,000 feet the speed would have been nearly 746 MPH, the speed of sound (at sea level). If this had been a large jet airplane "breaking the sound barrier" the witnesses might have heard a sonic boom even though the plane would have been about 13 miles away. Instead, on this quiet night with no wind, they heard nothing.

Misidentified Airplane Glint?

The only conventional non-hoax explanation for this sighting is that the witnesses misidentified an airplane. However, the airplane hypothesis is not without its problems. It must answer the questions, why didn't the witnesses hear the aircraft, why couldn't they see any wings and why did it appear, oddly enough, as two whitish ellipses with a darker, bluish area between?

As a possible answer to the last question, Jeffrey Sainio, MUFON image analyst, has pointed out that a glint (a very bright reflection of the sun) off the fuselage, the center of which was blocked from direct view by the wing closest to the observers, could appear as two bright objects with a dark space between. The answers to the first and second

questions then follow from the glint hypothesis: the airplane was so far away that the wings and other portions of the airplane were not visible (even though the bright glints were visible) and the sound was too faint for them to hear.

This explanation is based upon the idea that a glint actually occurred. It also assumes that the nearest wing blocked the direct view of the center of the fuselage, thus creating two approximately equal sized areas, to the front and back of the wing, which made the white images. Since it appears that the object(s) was flying along a level and straight trajectory, i.e., a hypothetical airplane was not turning left or "banking" with its left wing downward, this explanation also requires that the wing be attached at the bottom of the fuselage so that it could be between an observer on the ground and the main body (sides) of the fuselage. It just so happens that many models of aircraft have the fuselage "riding" on top of the wing. For these aircraft, the wing could obstruct the ground-level view of part of the fuselage even when the plane is flying level. If one assumes that this type of aircraft was flying past the witnesses, then one may propose the hypothesis that the two white images were glints from the front and rear portions of the fuselage while the nearest wing blocked the direct view of the center portion.

REFLECTION ANGLE REQUIRED TO CAUSE A GLINT

The glint or optimum reflection from a flat mirror (specular) surface takes place at a particular angle that satisfies the well-known reflection rule: angle of reflection (the "specular reflection angle") equals the angle of incidence. A non-specular (i.e., diffuse) but nevertheless smooth or "shiny" surface will reflect light over a wide range of angles, but the reflection will be brightest only over a small range of angles (a few degrees) centered about the specular reflection angle. The amplitude of the reflection will decrease considerably as the angle is tilted away from the specular reflection angle.

The glint hypothesis requires a particular alignment between the sun, the assumed airplane and the observers. The sun was at an angular elevation of about 5 degrees and an azimuth of about 297 degrees (according to the Expert Astronomer computer program). That is, the sun was about 27 degrees north of due west. As nearly as can be determined the axis of the assumed fuselage was at an azimuth angle of about 17 degrees measured as rotation clockwise from due north. Therefore, if the sun had been 17 degrees north of due west the sun rays would have been at an angle of 90 degrees (perpendicular) to the axis and the (specular) reflection angle would also have been 90 degrees to the axis. However, since the sun was 27 degrees north of due west, the sun rays were hitting the assumed fuselage at an angle of 90 - (27-17) = 80 degrees measured as counterclockwise rotation from the direction the assumed airplane was traveling, i.e., from the 17 degree azimuth. This is the incident angle. The angle of reflection would be the same, 80 degrees from the axis, but measured as clockwise rotation from the direction opposite to the direction the airplane was traveling, i.e., 80 degrees measured clockwise starting at the 197 degree azimuth. The brightest glint would occur at this angle of reflection. Thus the brightest rays from the glint would be traveling along an azimuth of 197+80 = 277 degrees as measured at the location of the assumed airplane. Recall that the direction from the observers to the object(s) was at an azimuth of about 70 degrees as the object(s) passed the steeple. The direction opposite to this 70 degree azimuth is the direction that reflected rays would have to travel from the assumed airplane to reach the observers. The opposite direction is 180 + 70 = 250 degrees. This is 27 degrees less than the azimuth for maximum glint, 277 degrees, calculated above. In other words, the observers' viewing location was 27 degrees away from the direction for an optimum glint, too far for the glint to be much, if any, brighter than the ordinary diffuse reflection from the assumed fuselage.

If Glint, Not From an Airplane

Fred saw the object(s) initially at an azimuth of about 125 degrees and he saw (videotaped) it again over the azimuth range from about 75 1/2 degrees to about 65 1/2 degrees. In other words, he saw it coming and going as it traveled in a straight line over a wide range in angles. A glint could not persist over such an angle range. Even within the relatively narrow range of about 10 degrees of azimuth captured on video one would expect a continual decrease in the glint brightness if there had been a glint. However, the only changes are several instances where the brightness decreases and returns to the full value as the object(s) is obscured by clouds. The size of the angle away from the expected glint direction combined with the lack of brightness variation attributable to alignment with the sun rules out glints from an airplane fuselage. If these images are glints, then they are glints from circular or elliptical objects, for which there is always some portion of the surface that satisfies the reflection rule.

DID A WING BLOCK
THE VIEW OF THE FUSELAGE?

The hypothesis that two white images could be created by a wing blocking the view of the center of a fuselage could be valid even without a glint. This would be based on the normal reflection from the fuselage under viewing conditions in which the wings, for some reason, could not be distinguished from the blue sky background. However, in this case the explanation of the failure to detect the wings could not be based, as before, on the assumption of a great distance to the airplane (with the consequent large size and speed). Under this hypothesis, as the plane traveled in a straight line past the observer the wing would first block the rear of the fuselage (as it approaches). Then the blocked area would move toward the front as the plane continued to fly past the observer. At some angle between the azimuth of the line of sight and the axis of the aircraft the wing would block the center of the fuselage. The size of this angle would depend upon the location of the wing attachment to the fuselage and also whether the wing was swept back or sticking straight out from the fuselage. Some aircraft have the wing attached forward of the center of the fuselage, some at the center and some have the wing attached behind the center. For the particular situation of this video, the assumed aircraft was viewed from the rear with the angle ranging from about 47 to about 57 degrees between the axis of the fuselage and the azimuth of the sighting direction. Under these viewing circumstances a wing that sticks straight out from the fuselage might block the front portion from direct view, but it wouldn't block the center portion. Thus it might create a single bright image, but not two equal bright areas. However, an aircraft with a narrow (not wide like on some fighter jets) swept back wing attached at about the center of the fuselage, such as on a Boeing 727, 747 or a Lockheed 1011, could block the view of the center of the fuselage while not blocking the front or rear portions. (Small passenger aircraft [Beechcraft, Piper] have the wings at the center of and perpendicular to the fuselage and thus do not satisfy this "swept-back" requirement.) The swept back wings on these aircraft make an angle of about 50 degrees with the fuselage. Therefore if the witnesses had been looking at one of these aircraft they would been looking at the nearest wing "end-on," but from below. However, to create the overall image length recorded on the videotape, a 727 (153 feet long), 747 (230 feet long) or 1011 (178 feet long) would have to have been so far away that it would have been exceeding the speed of sound, which they cannot do. So, the object(s) was not a large jet aircraft. Some fighter jets (50 - 65 feet long) also have swept-back wings. To make the image size recorded on video one of these aircraft would have to be about 4 miles away. However, the wings on these aircraft are very wide and block most

or all of the view of the rear half of the fuselage so there would again be only a single bright image of the front of the fuselage. Furthermore, it is quite likely that the witnesses would have heard the sound of a fighter jet only 4 - 5 miles away.

NEARBY SMALL AIRCRAFT HYPOTHESIS TESTED

Since the glint explanation, with its accompanying assumption of great distance to a large airplane, is rejected, then the assumed aircraft must have been reasonably close (within several miles). In this case the most important reason for rejecting the aircraft explanation is the lack of any indications of wings. Fred and his wife have said they could see no wings on the object(s) even though they saw it over a wider range of angles than is represented in the video. The video images are small, but they support this claim. The right hand inset in Figure 2 shows a comparison image constructed to look the way a typical T-shaped airplane would look if flying along the same path as the object(s). The comparison was constructed with the projected "fuselage" length equal to the overall length of the image of the object(s). This projection was carried out under the assumption that the wingspan, tip-to-tip, was approximately equal to the length of the fuselage, which is typical for aircraft that are not designed for supersonic flight. As can be seen from the comparison "airplane" image, if the object(s) had been an airplane seen at the same angular elevation and direction of travel relative to the sighting azimuth the wings would have been visible as protrusions above and below the image of the fuselage.

Although the diagram shows the situation for a T shaped aircraft, the same situation would occur for a large aircraft with swept back wings or a high performance jet (fighter): The outer end of the nearest wing would be silhouetted against the sky above the fuselage and the farthest wing would be silhouetted against the sky below the fuselage. Fred has demonstrated that his camera could have detected wings under roughly comparable viewing conditions by videotaping objects known to be aircraft. The wings are clearly visible. The image of the object(s) has no indications of wing-like protrusions.

Figure 2 also has several blowups of the image. These are representative of roughly four dozen other images for which wings should be apparent if the object(s) were an aircraft. These blowups also show that the spacing between the white images appears to be blue or pale blue, as if some of the white color from the elliptical images was "spilling over" into the darker blue area. Such "spillage" is common for optoelectronic systems

such as video cameras, and so may be expected here. Over the five or so degree range of azimuth angles for which there are good images there seems to be little change in the size, location, bluish color or brightness of the dark space between the white ellipses. If the dark space were the result of a wing blocking the direct view of the fuselage, the space between the two white reflections would not appear to have the blue sky color. Instead it would have a darker version of the same color as the elliptical images (unless the color of the bottom of the wing were different from that of the fuselage).

AIRCRAFT HYPOTHESIS REJECTED

For all the reasons cited, then, the image is not consistent with what would be expected if the object(s) was an aircraft. On the other hand, it is consistent with what might be expected if two elliptical objects, white in color, close together and either connected by a small appendage or entirely separate, traveled at a moderate speed and moderate altitude (5 - 10,000 feet) past the witnesses. In this height range each object would have been 8 - 16 feet in diameter.

NOT A HOAX

The MUFON investigation indicates that this was not a hoax since the witnesses are upstanding citizens of the community, are both employed in law-enforcement at a state prison in New York and have requested anonymity.

COMPARISON WITH OTHER SIGHTINGS

Since the aircraft and hoax explanations are ruled out, the image can be considered to be that of a single unidentified flying object with two major whitish sections connected by a narrow structure not seen on the video or of two whitish elliptical unidentified flying objects traveling in a close formation. By way of comparison, the statistical study carried out by the Battelle Memorial Institute under contract to the Air Force (Project 10073, Special Report #14, May 1955, published by the Air Technical Intelligence Center, Wright-Patterson Air Force Base) carefully studied 3201 sightings (designated as "All Sightings") reported between January 1947 and the end of December, 1952. They determined that 689 sightings (21.5% of the total) were unexplained after analysis. Of these, 177 (26% of the unknowns) were of white or "glowing white" objects, 331 (48% of the unknowns) were elliptical, 64 sightings (9%) involved two objects (150 involved more than 3 objects), 56 sightings (8%) lasted 11-30 seconds and 61 (9%) lasted 31 to 60 seconds. A direct comparison between these statistics and this sighting cannot be made since the Battelle study did not distinguish between daytime sightings of white ellipses and nighttime sightings of glowing white objects. A closer comparison can be made with the statistics presented in *The UFO Evidence* (Hall, 1964; soon to be republished) which show that of 253 daytime or twilight sightings for which color was reported, 81 or 32% were white objects and of 333 sightings for which shape was given, 173 (51%) were round or elliptical. These statistics show that the sightings of fraction of the totality of UFO sightings. In other words, except for the video, this sighting is far from being a unique event.

The calculations presented above are based on the assumption that the axis of the object(s) was in a horizontal plane. If the axis were not in a horizontal plane, i.e., if the object(s) were traveling upwards or downwards, then these numerical values of length and speed would have to be revised somewhat depending upon the angle of tilt. Hence these lengths and speeds must be considered approximations to the actual size and speed of the object(s) for any given assumed height, but must not be considered definitive.

I thank Fred and his wife for providing the original video along with calibrations for the analysis and videos of various aircraft for comparison purposes. I also thank Jim Bouck for help in interviewing the witnesses and making measurements at the site and Jeffrey Sainio for valuable comments on the analysis of the images.

Note: After the preceding analysis was published in the *MUFON Journal* in January, 1999, I was been informed by John Thompson of a February 1997 sighting in LaGrange, Georgia, involving a sheriff and other witnesses who saw a similar or identical object. They took one picture which shows an object that appears identical to the one videotaped by Fred. The sighting in Georgia had not been publicized at the time of the sighting discussed here, nor was I made aware of the Georgia sighting until several months after this analysis had been completed. For details on the Georgia case and a view of the photo see www. isur.com and click on "UFO Photo Case, LaGrange, Ga."

For a number of years, certain questions have recurred concerning the origin of these UFO crafts. Are they solid objects that travel through space, are they interdimensional crafts, or are they from here on Earth? They may be all three, or something else altogether.

ENDNOTES

1 (source "Mysteries of The Unexplained" by *Reader's Digest* p.217 – 218 and *The UFO Book* by Jerome Clark, p. 342 –345)
2 John G. Fuller's book *THE INTERRUPTED JOURNEY* (Berkley, 1966)
3 Associated Press articles in the book *UFOs A Pictorial History from Antiquity to Present* by Davis C. Knight
4 *Left At East Gate* by Larry Warren and Peter Robbins
5 *The UFO Experience* by J. Allen Hynek p. 165 – 167
6 *National Enquirer,* 4/21/68
7 *National Enquirer,* 4/21/68
8 *Bangor Daily News,* March 28, 1966
9 *National Enquirer,* 4/21/68
10 *Cincinnati Post* and *Cincinnati Enquirer*, 4/17/68
11 *Schenectady Gazette* newspaper
12 Ibid
13 *Schenectady Gazette,* 10/19/73
14 *Mobile Register* newspaper, 10/9/73
15 *Mobile Register* newspaper, 10/9/73
16 *Hudson Valley Magazine* (CUFOS investigations)
17 *National Enquirer* newspaper, 10/22/74
18 *National Enquirer,* 12/31/74
19 *Celestial Passengers*, by Margaret Sachs and Ernest Jahn
20 *National Enquirer,* 5/6/75
21 *National Enquirer,* 11/12/1974
22 *National Enquirer,* 6/10/75
23 *National Enquirer,* 9/9/75
24 *National Enquirer,* 3/2/76
25 *National Enquirer,* 3/30/76
26 *National Enquirer*, 6/15/76
27 *National Enquirer*, 6/29/76,
28 *Schenectady Gazette*, 8/26/76
29 *Hudson Valley* magazine (MUFON investigation)
30 Files of R. Bonefant, independent investigator
31 *Kentucky Post*, 1/20/78
32 *Albany Times Union*
33 *Pursuit* magazine, 1979 winter issue
34 MUFON Investigation
35 Youtube video of History Channel submitted by Denny from space
36 *Night Siege: The Hudson Valley Sightings* by Dr. J Allen Hynek, Philip Imbrogno and Bob Pratt
37 MUFON Investigation
38 NUFORC website
39 http://illinoismufon.com/mufon_015.htm
40 http://hine.fuse.net/ufo/willoughvy04.html and NUFORC
41 http://www.empiretribune.com/articles/2008/01/11/news/news01.txt
42 http://www.npr.org/templates/story/story.php?storyId=18146244 and http://www.associatedcontent.com/article/542887/ufo_sighting_near_stephenville_texas.html
43 *National Enquirer*, 4/8/75
44 *UFO Magazine* Press Archives
45 Ibid

46 http://pgrsel.100megs13.com/times24oct67.htm
47 http://pgrsel.100megs13.com/press/diarioleregaiao3aug.77.htm
48 http://pgrsel.100megs13.com/press/l'alsace20sep1998.htm
49 http://www.lavozdelpueblo.com.ar/diario/2007-11-10/La_Region/24309.htm
50 http://pgrsel.100megs13.com/press/francesoir13sep1995.htm
51 http://members.tripod.com/Royce3/Writers/Jeff_Love/Articles/articles_21.htm
52 *Schenectady Gazette*, 3/13/80
53 Lecture by Michael Nelson at the 2007 MUFON Symposium in Denver, Colorado
54 *Schenectady Gazette* 11/14/73
55 *Albany Times Union* Newspaper and a radio interview on WGY between John Wallace Spencer and one of the Air traffic controllers.
56 *Incident at Exeter* by Robert G. Fuller
57 Ibid
58 Personal interview with witness
59 Personal interview with the witness
60 *UFOs and the National Security State* by Richard Dolan
61 Ibid
62 *UFOs and the National Security State*, by R. Dolan and *The UFO Book* by J. Clark
63 NASA Channel on TV
64 *UFOs and the National Security State* by Richard Dolan
65 alien-ufo-research.com/astronaut_ufo_sightings
66 Ibid
67 Ibid
68 Ibid
69 Ibid
70 Ibid
71 *The UFO Book Encyclopedia of the Extraterrestrial* by Jerome Clark
72 Ibid
73 *UFOs and the National Security State* by R. Dolan and The UFO Book by Jerome Clark
74 presidentialufo.com
75 Ibid
76 Ibid
77 Ibid
78 *UFOs and the National Security State* by Richard Dolan, pages 393 and 394
79 From the DVD *UFO: Top Secret* as seen on Sci-Fi and TLC channels
80 presidentialufo.com
81 Ibid
82 *Flying Saucer, Serious Business* by Frank Edwards
83 Presidentialufo.com
84 *The UFO Book Encyclopedia of the Extraterrestrial*
85 *Witnessed*, by Budd Hopkins Albany, New York

PLACES INDEX

MEMORIAL
BUDD HOPKINS
6/15/31 - 8/21/11

AUGUST 22, 2011 12:30 A.M.

My friend and fellow co-writer, Jim Bouck called me with the stunning sad news that Budd Hopkins had passed away.

I just could not register this information so I asked Jim, "What did you say?"

Jim repeated, "Budd Hopkins is dead."

Sat. May 10, 2003
Jim Bouck, Frank Soriano, Budd Hopkins author of " Intruders & Witnessed "

I felt nauseated combined with a sadness of the important loss for myself as well as the world. Budd opened many doors to and about the strange, yet real, world of UFOs and its contents. This pioneer was a first in many aspects of the UFO phenomena and time will prove him right. He helped many with their encounters and the aftermath; that also includes this writer.

Thank you Budd.

~Frank Soriano

For every one who knew Budd Hopkins, and those who didn't have that privilege, Budd had done much to open the doors of knowledge and to provide the strength needed to handle this enigma.

Thank you Budd, God bless you and rest in peace.

~Jim Bouck